W9-CLI-835

MAPPING
AND
NAVIGATION

Explore the History and Science of Finding Your Way

with 20 Projects

Cynthia Light Brown and Patrick M. McGinty
Illustrated by Beth Hetland

~ Latest titles in the *Build It Yourself* Series ~

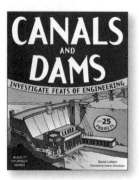
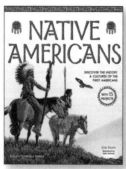
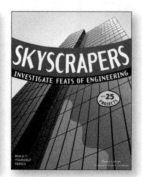
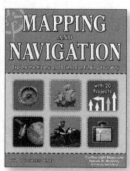

Check out more titles at www.nomadpress.net

Nomad Press
A division of Nomad Communications
10 9 8 7 6 5 4 3 2 1

This book was manufactured by Sheridan Books, Ann Arbor, MI USA.
October 2013, Job #350759
ISBN: 978-1-61930-194-8

Illustrations by Beth Hetland
Educational Consultant, Marla Conn

Questions regarding the ordering of this book should be addressed to
Nomad Press
2456 Christian St.
White River Junction, VT 05001
www.nomadpress.net

Nomad Press is committed to preserving ancient forests and natural resources.
We elected to print *Mapping and Navigation: Explore the History and Science of
Finding Your Way* on Thor PCW containing 30% post consumer waste.

Nomad Press made this paper choice because our printer, Sheridan Books, is a member of
Green Press Initiative, a nonprofit program dedicated to supporting authors, publishers,
and suppliers in their efforts to reduce their use of fiber obtained from endangered forests.

For more information, visit **www.greenpressinitiative.org**.

CONTENTS

BCE

1400s BCE: the Chinese start using a grid system to lay out their cities.

500s BCE: a Babylonian map called the Imago Mundi is created showing the world as seven islands surrounding Babylon and the Euphrates River. This is in what is modern-day Iraq.

300s BCE: the Qin dynasty in China makes the first grid maps.

200s BCE: Eratosthenes, the first person to use the word *geography*, calculates the earth's circumference to be about 24,390 miles (36,250 kilometers). He draws a map of the known world using lines of latitude and longitude.

200s BCE: Pei Xiu uses a grid system to show Chinese cities.

100–300s CE

120 CE: maps made by Marinus of Tyre are the first in the Roman Empire to show China.

150 CE: Claudius Ptolemy, a Roman citizen living in Egypt, publishes *Geographia*, which contains a huge list of the names of cities and their locations on a grid system. He also develops detailed maps using latitude and longitude.

300s CE: the Peutinger Map shows the road networks, bodies of water, and settlements in the Roman Empire, as well as distances between cities.

1400–1500s

1487: Bartholomew Dias (Portugal) discovers the southern tip of Africa.

1492: Christopher Columbus (Italy) discovers the New World.

1497: John Cabot (Italy) discovers Newfoundland, Canada.

1497–1499: Vasco da Gama (Portugal) discovers a water route between Portugal and India.

1502: Amerigo Vespucci (Italy) explores the New World.

1507: the Waldseemüller Map is the first map to use America as the name for the New World, named after explorer Amerigo Vespucci.

1513: Juan Ponce de León (Spain) discovers Florida on his search for the Fountain of Youth.

1513: Vasco Núñez de Balboa (Spain) crosses the Isthmus of Panama and is the first European to see the Pacific Ocean from its eastern shore.

1519–1522: Ferdinand Magellan (Portugal) sails around the world.

1540: Francisco Vásquez de Coronado (Spain) is the first European to explore the American Southwest in Arizona and New Mexico.

1569: Gerardus Mercator makes his famous map of the world called the Mercator projection.

↙ TIMELINE ↘

1600–1700s

1608: The first telescopes are invented by Hans Lippershey, Zacharias Janssen, and Jacob Metius.

1609: Galileo Galilei is the first person to use a telescope to observe the heavens.

1620: Dutch architect Cornelius Drebel constructs the first submarine. He tests it in the Thames River in England.

1643: Evangelista Torricelli develops the first working barometer.

1668: Isaac Newton invents the first reflecting telescope.

1757: John Bird makes the first sextant.

1773: John Harrison is awarded the prize for inventing the marine chronometer, which tells accurate time at sea and allows for determination of longitude.

1783: the Montgolfier brothers of France launch unmanned flights in a hot air balloon. The first free flight with human passengers soon follows.

1800s

1803: Lewis and Clark set off from Pittsburgh, Pennsylvania, on the Corps of Discovery Expedition to explore and map the western United States.

1804: Sir George Cayley of Great Britain flies the first model glider.

1807: President Thomas Jefferson authorizes the Survey of the Coast, which is the first attempt to map the ocean in an organized system.

1855: U.S. Navy Lieutenant Matthew Maury publishes a map that is the first to show underwater mountains in the mid-Atlantic Ocean.

1856: Jean-Marie Le Bris of France makes the first flight that goes higher than his point of departure by having a horse pull him on a beach.

1869: John Wesley Powell leads an expedition down the Colorado River to map the Grand Canyon.

1872: The HMS *Challenger* circumnavigates the globe on a four-year voyage that discovers 4,417 new marine creatures.

1891: Otto Lilienthal of Germany is the first to successfully pilot gliders in flight.

1896: Samuel P. Langley of the United States flies a steam-powered model plane.

1900s

1903: Orville and Wilbur Wright of the United States make the first engine-powered, heavier-than-air flight near Kitty Hawk, North Carolina. The flight goes about 120 feet and lasts 12 seconds.

1906: Lewis Nixon invents the first sonar device to detect icebergs.

1921: the first flight to carry airmail crosses the United States.

1926: Robert Goddard (United States) launches the first liquid-fueled rocket.

1928: Amelia Earhart is the first woman to cross the Atlantic Ocean by airplane.

1930: William Beebe and Otis Barton dive 1,430 feet in their steel submersible called the *Bathysphere*.

1932: Jan Oort finds evidence for the existence of dark matter in space.

1932: Amelia Earhart is the first woman and second person ever to fly solo across the Atlantic Ocean.

1935: Amelia Earhart is the first person to fly solo between California and Hawaii.

1937: Amelia Earhart attempts to fly around the world along the equator. Her plane disappears over the Pacific Ocean during the final legs of the flight.

1942: Germany launches the V-2 rocket, which is the first vehicle to cross into outer space.

1957: *Sputnik 1*, the first artificial satellite, is launched by the Soviet Union (now Russia).

1960: Jacques Piccard and Don Walsh dive to the deepest point in the Mariana Trench, 6.6 miles below the surface.

1961: Yuri Gagarin (Soviet Union) is the first human to enter space.

1962: The United States launches *Mariner 2* to fly past Venus, which is the first flyby.

1969: Neil Armstrong (United States) is the first human to walk on the moon.

1971: *Salyut 1*, from the Soviet Union, is the first space station.

1972: the United States Air Force conducts test flights with experimental GPS receivers, the type that could be used in a satellite navigation system.

1972: the United States launches Landsat satellite.

1978: the United States launches the first GPS satellite.

1983: U.S. President Ronald Reagan announces that GPS will be available for civilian use.

1990: the Hubble Space Telescope takes pictures while orbiting the earth.

1998: dark energy is discovered and the first evidence that the universe's expansion is speeding up.

2000s

2000: civilians are allowed access to the same accuracy as military GPS.

2012: the most recent GPS satellite is launched on October 4.

2012: the Hubble Space Telescope discovers seven galaxies over 13 billion light years away, including one that is 13.3 billion light years away.

Finding Your Way

How do you find your way from one place to another? You probably don't think about it, but you practice **navigation** skills every day to do this. How do you get from your house to the bus stop? How do you get to classrooms around your school? You **navigate** there! When you navigate, you are planning or following a route from one place to another.

W🔴rds2Know

navigation: figuring out locations and planning or following routes.

navigate: to make your way from one place to another on water, air, or land, especially in a ship, aircraft, or vehicle.

Words 2 Know

navigator: a person or device that navigates.

cartographer: a person who makes maps.

GPS: stands for Global Positioning System. The system of **satellites**, computers, and **receivers** can determine the exact location of a receiver anywhere on the planet. It is used to determine location, speed, and direction.

satellite: an object that circles another object in space. Also a device that circles the earth and transmits information.

receiver: a device that converts signals such as radio waves into sound or visual form.

atlas: a book of maps or charts.

Look around. You'll see **navigators** on foot, in cars, on bikes, and in trains. Bus drivers navigate routes to deliver riders. People driving cars are navigating from one place to another. And don't forget to look up where you might see pilots navigating the skies.

We usually know how to get where we want to go. You probably know the way to school, a friend's house, or the library. But what happens when we need help finding our way? We use a map!

Putting the World on the Page

Ever since people first drew on cave walls, we have used maps to try to understand our world. **Cartographers** are experts at making maps to represent the world. At first they did this by hand and with very little information. Now cartographers have computers and other equipment to make their maps more accurate and full of details. Whether it's a map that pops up on a **GPS** screen, or a road **atlas** you page through in your car, all maps help us find our way.

2

Most maps today share several features. If you have one handy, take it out to see if yours has these features, too.

Legend: A **legend** shows what the different symbols on the map mean. It's like a dictionary for your map. It might show that a black dot on the map stands for a city or that a blue line stands for a river.

Scale: Usually near the bottom of a map, you'll find a **scale** that tells how many inches or centimeters on the map equal how many miles or kilometers in real life. It might use a bar scale, showing an inch and the number of miles represented, or it might say something like "1 inch = 5 miles." The scale might even show a ratio like 1:250,000, which means that one unit of distance on the map equals 250,000 of the same units on the ground.

Words 2 Know

legend: a key to all the symbols used on a map.

scale: the ratio of a distance on the map to the corresponding distance on the ground.

North arrow: Somewhere on a map is an arrow with a capital N. This points north. North is usually at the top of the paper, but not always. For example, maps of the Arctic region are often centered on the North Pole, so north is in the center, and south points outward toward all of the edges.

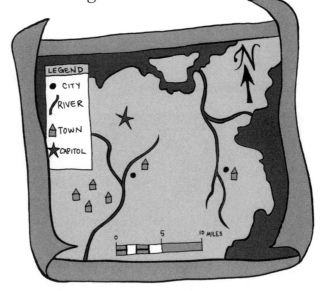

3

Types of Maps

The most common types of maps are road maps. They show how roads stretch across cities and states and connect with other roads.

But there are other kinds of maps you may not know about. **Topographic maps** show the manmade and natural features of the land and changes in **elevation**. They use **contour lines** to tell us how tall a mountain is or how low a valley dips. You can think of *topo* or topographic maps as representing everything on "top" of the land.

WOrds2Know

topographic map: a map that uses large-scale detail to show both natural and man-made features, usually including elevation.

elevation: the height above sea level.

contour lines: lines on a map that show changes in elevation.

magnet: something that attracts metal.

DID YOU KNOW?

The star design on a map is called a compass rose. A compass is a device that uses a **magnet** to show which direction is north. A compass rose is like a picture of a compass with the different directions marked. These are sometimes very simple with just an "N," or they can get very fancy with beautiful designs and labels for north, south, east, west, northeast, northwest, southeast, southwest, and more!

Other types of maps show useful information like **climate**, **vegetation**, or population. These maps often use colors or shade patterns to show differences. For instance, a rainfall map of the United States would use one color for the wet and rainy Pacific Northwest and another for the hot and dry Desert Southwest.

Technology: The Key to Making Better Maps

How do mapmakers know how tall to make mountains on their topo maps? How do they know how much rain falls in a region? All of these maps are made possible because of **technology**. But technology isn't just electronic gadgets like cell phones and laptops. Even the development of paper for making maps was new technology at one time. The history of mapmaking is full of remarkable people who **charted** the unknown with an ever-changing set of tools.

Whether using 20-foot-long maps (6 meters) or GPS devices that fit in our palms, mapmakers have always tried to build a better representation of the world. It's hard to imagine how much is still out there to discover!

In this book you'll learn about great navigators throughout history and how we make maps and navigate today. Along the way, you'll find fun and interesting facts, and you'll get to do experiments and projects to help you understand the concepts even better.

W🔵rds2Know

climate: average weather patterns in an area over a long period of time.

vegetation: all the plant life in an area.

technology: tools, methods, and systems used to solve a problem or do work.

chart: to make a map or detailed plan.

ACTIVITY

MAKE YOUR OWN
*M*AP OF *Y*OUR *N*EIGHBORHOOD

SUPPLIES

✳ sheets of paper
✳ colored pencils
✳ ruler
✳ tape
✳ measuring tape
✳ compass

1 Draw a map of your neighborhood or your school and its surroundings. Use one colored pencil for streets, and different colors for other objects such as houses, other buildings, or parks. If you want straight lines, use the ruler. Attach sheets of paper together with the tape if you need more space.

2 For objects like houses or trees, draw a small picture or shape each time, called a symbol. Make a legend for your map showing each symbol and what it represents.

3 Measure the length of your house using the measuring tape. To figure out the scale of your map, compare the length of your house to the length of your house on paper. If your house is 30 feet long (9 meters), and you drew it as 1 inch long (2½ centimeters), your scale will be 1 inch = 30 feet (1 centimeter = 9 meters). Write the scale in the legend or show it using a bar scale.

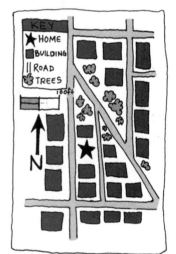

4 Figure out which way is north using a compass. Draw the north arrow somewhere on your map, or even a full compass rose!

What's Happening?

A map of a fairly small area like your neighborhood is sometimes called a plan. It is also called a large-scale map because it zooms in on a small area to show a lot of detail. What do you think your street might look like on a map of your entire city? What about on a map of your state?

↗ CHAPTER 1 ↖

Ancient Maps

Long before people had written languages, they began
drawing maps. Early maps were simple compared with
the maps we have today. Some of the first maps just
showed hills and rivers. As mapmaking developed,
maps of regions showed roads and cities, but these
maps weren't especially accurate because people
didn't have the right tools to measure distance and
direction. Many ancient maps, especially ones of the
world or the stars, were symbolic. This means the
maps were made more to get across an idea than
to be exact, so they did not focus on the details.

People from ancient **cultures** couldn't travel as far or communicate as easily with other cultures as we can today. This meant they often couldn't share their mapmaking strategies either. So the history of mapmaking and navigation in the ancient world moves at different speeds in different parts of the world. Sometimes, people in different cultures were working on the same mapmaking methods at the same time without knowing it.

WOrds 2 Know

culture: a group of people and their beliefs and way of life.

grid system: a type of city plan in which streets run at right angles to each other, forming a grid.

perimeter: the length of the line around something.

DID YOU KNOW?

The Babylonian Map of the World, called the *Imago Mundi*, is the first surviving map of the world. Today this area is in modern-day Iraq. The map was drawn on clay tablets more than 2,500 years ago. It was a symbolic map, showing Babylon at the center surrounded by water and islands. Three of the islands are named "place of the rising sun," "the sun is hidden and nothing can be seen," and "beyond the flight of birds."

Early Compasses and Grid Systems in China

To learn about many of the first navigational technologies, look to Chinese history. Chinese cities were among the first to be planned out using a **grid system**. You've probably used grid paper in math class to plot lines or figure out the **perimeter** of a shape.

Sometimes city streets are designed to cross like the lines of a grid. It makes a city easy to get around.

From as early as the fifteenth **century BCE**, the Chinese were interested in planning out their cities very carefully. Early Chinese writings state that "a capital city should be square on plan. Three gates on each side of the perimeter lead into the nine main streets that crisscross the city and define its grid pattern. And for its layout the city should have the Royal Court situated in the south, the Marketplace in the north."

WOrds2Know

century: 100 years.

BCE: put after a date, BCE stands for Before Common Era and counts down to zero. CE stands for Common Era and counts up from zero.

military: the armed forces of a country.

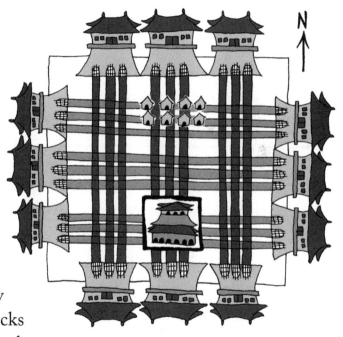

Since their cities were often preplanned, it made the work of Chinese cartographers easier. The Qin Dynasty developed the earliest known grid maps in the fourth century BCE. They were drawn on wooden blocks with black ink. These maps show rivers and roads as well as city names. They include surprising details such as where to find good lumber and distances between locations. These early maps were also some of the first topographic maps. Later, the Han Dynasty made more complicated maps on silk that covered large areas and listed things like population and **military** bases.

Pei Xiu and His Six Principles of Mapping

Pei Xiu was a Chinese cartographer in the third century BCE. While grid systems had existed in Chinese city planning for centuries, Xiu was the first to accurately show them on maps. His writings discuss six ways to deal with problems of distance, direction, and scale that he wanted included on all future maps.

* A scale to understand the size of an area.

* A rectangular grid to organize the scale.

* Accurate **pacing** to determine the distance between two locations.

* Ways to show height or elevation.

* Ways to show the **slope** of a land feature.

* Ways to measure curves and represent them on maps.

WOrds 2 Know

pacing: measuring a distance by walking it and counting the number of steps taken.

slope: the slant of a surface with one end higher than another.

compass: a device that uses a magnet to show which direction is north.

There is a kind of rock called lodestone that is a natural magnet. It always lines up pointing in the north and south direction. In ancient China, people placed a lodestone on a metal plate and watched as it lined up with a picture on the plate that they believed told their future. Soon people realized that lodestones could do more than point to fortunes. Around 200 BCE the Chinese began using lodestones to develop the world's first **compasses**.

DID YOU KNOW?

The Lascaux Caves in southwestern France are famous for their paintings of large animals, painted over 17,000 years ago. The caves also contain clusters of dots, which some researchers think are actually maps of stars!

For the next thousand years, the Chinese experimented with magnets and compasses. It's difficult to know exactly when certain developments took place, but in ancient Chinese writings, **scholars** knew that lodestones attract iron. They mention south pointers and mysterious needles. They created a ladle-shaped compass of lodestone whose handle pointed south on a plate of bronze. Eventually, Chinese scholars discovered how to magnetize needles to make **wet compasses**. They noticed that a magnetized needle floating in a bowl of water would swing around to point north. By 1100 CE, the needle became the centerpiece of the compass, and ship navigators had a valuable tool to help them sail the seas.

W○**rds?**

scholar: a person who highly educated in a subject.

wet compass: a compass formed with a magnetic needle floating in water.

landmark: a manmade or natural object that is easily seen from a distance and can be used to find or mark a location.

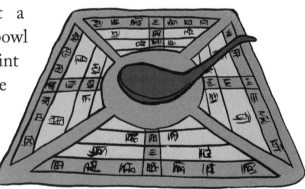

Egyptians: Guided by Stars

Navigating your way through a city can be difficult, but there is help all around you. If you get lost, you can look at street signs, **landmarks**, or ask for directions. You can look at a map. But what would you do without maps? What if there were no signs? What if you were lost at sea with only water and sky all around? How did ancient sailors navigate without a clear path before them?

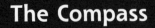

The Compass

Words 2 Know

pole: one end of a magnet.

repel: to resist or push away.

magnetic field: the invisible area around a magnet that pulls objects to it or pushes them away.

axis of rotation: an imaginary line through a planet's poles, around which it rotates.

A compass is a navigational tool that shows direction. It has a small, lightweight magnet called a needle that spins freely on a pin. One end of the needle always points north. It is usually painted red or marked with an "N." But why does the needle point north?

You probably know from using magnets that opposite **poles** attract and like poles **repel**. This is key to what makes a compass work. Picture a giant bar magnet buried in the middle of the earth like an apple core. This magnet has a north and a south pole. Like all magnets, it has a **magnetic field** around it. A compass needle is also magnetic. This makes the south end of the needle turn toward its opposite pole—the north. So the pointed end of the needle labeled with an N is actually its south end. That's why it's attracted to the north end of the magnet.

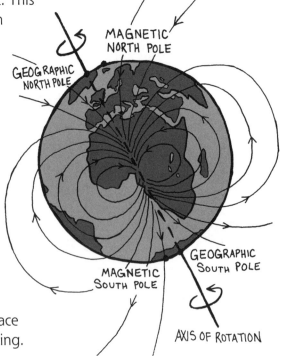

A compass points to the magnetic North Pole, which is the point on the earth's surface where the magnetic field points straight down. This is different from the geographic North Pole that we think of as the top of a globe. The geographic North Pole is the northernmost point on the earth, where the earth's **axis of rotation** meets the surface. These are not in the same place because the magnetic North Pole is always shifting.

WOrds2Know

astronomer: a person who studies objects in the sky such as the sun, moon, planets, and stars.

constellation: a group of stars that form a recognizable pattern or design.

Polaris: the North Star, which is almost directly over the North Pole.

destination: the place to which you are going.

I SEE A SPOON!

NO, IT'S A BEAR!

Ancient Egyptians realized they could look up to the sun, moon, or stars to find their way. They noticed that the stars moved across the sky every night and that, depending on the time of year, the stars always followed the same path. Soon ancient Egyptian **astronomers** figured out paths for 36 different **constellations** of stars. They used them as both a map and a clock to track the distance and time of their travels.

Many cultures had long been able to locate **Polaris**, the North Star. But Egyptian astronomers first realized that their location made a difference in how high a star or constellation appeared in the sky. If you could stand at the North Pole, for instance, the North Star would be almost directly overhead. The farther south you travel, the lower in the sky it appears.

TRY THIS!

Stand directly below an overhead light and point at it. You'll be pointing straight up. Now move to the side a few steps while still pointing at the light. You'll be pointing at an angle. Egyptian sailors used approximate calculations like these to tell where they were in relation to Polaris and their **destination**.

WOrds 2 Know

equator: the imaginary line around the earth halfway between the North and South Poles. The line divides the world into the Northern and Southern Hemispheres.

latitude: a measure of distance from the equator, in degrees. The equator is 0 degrees. The North Pole is 90 degrees latitude north and the South Pole is 90 degrees latitude south.

parallel: when two lines going in the same direction can continue forever and never touch, like an = sign.

longitude: a measure of distance from the prime meridian, in degrees. The prime meridian is 0 degrees with lines running 180 degrees east and west from it.

prime meridian: the imaginary line running from the North Pole to the South Pole through Greenwich, England. The line divides the world into the Eastern and Western Hemispheres.

Middle Ages: the name for a period of time from around 500 to 1400 CE. It is also called the Medieval Era.

Over time, Egyptians came up with the concept of using imaginary lines on the earth's surface for the purpose of locating a specific place. Every globe has horizontal lines that run like belts north and south of the **equator**. These lines of **latitude** tell us how far north or south we are on the earth's surface.

You'll also see **parallel** lines that stripe the globe from top to bottom, meeting at the North Pole and the South Pole. These lines of **longitude** tell us how far east or west we are from the **prime meridian**. By the **Middle Ages**, latitude and longitude had become a common language among mapmakers and navigators.

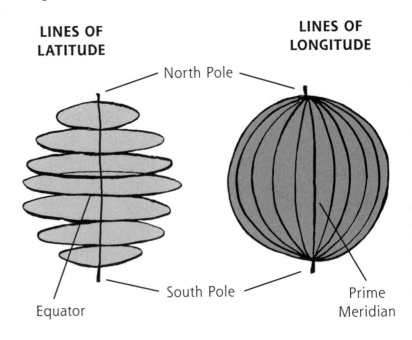

LINES OF LATITUDE

LINES OF LONGITUDE

North Pole

South Pole

Equator

Prime Meridian

W⊙rds2Know

geography: the study of the physical features of the earth and how human activity affects and is affected by these features.

universe: everything that exists everywhere.

circumference: the distance around something. The circumference of the earth is the distance around its widest point, called the equator.

Claudius Ptolemy is considered the father of **geography**. He lived in Egypt from about 85 to 165 CE, though he was actually Greek. Using Egyptian ideas about latitude and longitude, Ptolemy made remarkably accurate maps. He believed that the world was round, and that lines of latitude should be equally spaced from top to bottom on a globe. This is why lines of latitude are called parallels.

Lines of longitude, called meridians, were trickier. Ptolemy decided that they should all cross at the North and South Poles, meaning that the distance between meridians changes. At the equator, there is wider gap between lines of longitude than there is close to the North Pole. Ptolemy established the standard that north is at the top of a map and east to the right.

WHY NOT PUT **N**ORTH AT THE TOP?

While Ptolemy's work influenced astronomers and navigators for centuries, he mistakenly believed that the earth was at the center of the **universe**. He also miscalculated the **circumference** of the earth, estimating it to be only 18,000 miles (29,000 kilometers).

DID YOU KNOW?

The circle of the globe is divided into 360 parts. Each part is called a degree. Each degree is divided into 60 minutes and each minute is divided into 60 seconds.

15

Calculating the Earth's Circumference

How was it possible to calculate the circumference of the earth before anyone crossed the Atlantic Ocean? A brilliant mathematician and scientist, Eratosthenes, did just that in the third century BCE. He heard that on June 21 the sun didn't cast a shadow in Syene, Egypt. But where he lived, north of Syene in Alexandria, Egypt, the sun always cast a shadow. Eratosthenes knew that the farther you are from the equator, the lower the sun will be in the sky, and the longer shadows will be.

He measured the length of the shadow in Alexandria on June 21 and figured out that the sun was 7 degrees, 14 minutes, from overhead. That measurement is one-fiftieth of the 360 degrees that make up a circle. So he determined that the distance from Syene to Alexandria was one-fiftieth the distance around the earth. Eratosthenes also knew that camels took 50 days to travel from Syene to Alexandria, and he knew how fast camels traveled.

At that time, people used a different unit of measurement, called a stadium, for distance. Eratosthenes calculated the circumference of the earth to be about 252,000 stadia. That works out to be about 24,390 miles (39,250 kilometers), which is remarkably close to our measurements today of 24,855 miles (40,000 kilometers).

Greeks: Inventors of Tools

While the Chinese worked to get their grid systems recorded and the Egyptians mapped the stars in the sky, the Greeks were hard at work inventing tools to make both tasks easier. The Greeks created many technologies we use today, such as wheelbarrows, waterwheels, and alarm clocks.

A Greek invention you may not be familiar with is the **astrolabe**. Invented around 150 BCE, astrolabes were used to locate and predict the positions of the sun, moon, **planets**, and stars. They also helped establish a relationship between local time and local latitude by showing how the sky looks at a specific place and time.

On rough sea voyages, it was difficult to keep an astrolabe steady enough to make accurate measurements. So navigators made adjustments to create the mariner's astrolabe. Navigators held this astrolabe by a ring at the top and measured the angle between the **zenith** and a **celestial body** such as the North Star. Navigators aimed one pointer at the zenith and slid a moveable arm down to where they saw the celestial body. By counting the markings in between they could determine the angle. Christopher Columbus was extremely skilled with a mariner's astrolabe.

Ferdinand Magellan used his astrolabe to help him navigate around the world between 1519 and 1522.

Words 2 Know

astrolabe: a Greek instrument used to determine the position of the sun and stars.

planet: a large body in space with an **orbit** around the sun.

orbit: the path of an object circling another in space.

zenith: the point directly overhead in the sky.

celestial body: a star, planet, moon, or other object in the sky.

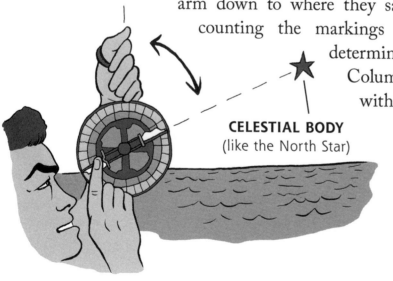

ZENITH

CELESTIAL BODY
(like the North Star)

Mappae Mundi

Toward the end of the Middle Ages, from around the eleventh century until the fifteenth century, European mapping became less accurate and more fanciful. The goal of mapping during this time was more for knowledge and religious instruction than for actual navigation. A map was called a mappa mundi, which means chart of the world. One map shows a creature called a Bonacon, which is like a bison with curled horns that sprays acidic dung. Another map shows the Sciapod of Greek mythology, who were people with enormous feet. On a globe made in 1507, the eastern coast of Asia is marked in Latin "HC SVNT DRACONES" which means, roughly, "Here Be Dragons."

On some ancient Chinese maps, certain cities would be shown as islands floating out in the sea. On others, lakes and mountains would be missing completely. New technologies would be needed to better represent the known world. And they'd be needed quickly, because the known world was about to expand.

HC SVNT DRACONES (Here Be Dragons)

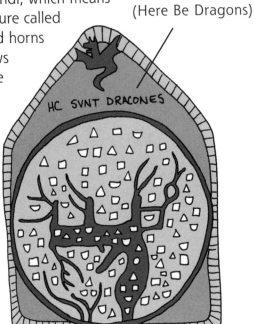

Roman Road Maps

The Romans put many of these Greek inventions to use. As the Roman Empire expanded, it became increasingly important to have good maps. They needed road maps for Roman soldiers. Most roads were shown as straight lines without any of the correct changes in direction, but the length was usually right.

The Peutinger Map is the Romans' only surviving map, but it is one of the most famous maps of the ancient world. It shows settlements, roads, rivers, and bodies of water and lists the distances between cities. Three cities, Rome, Constantinople, and Antioch, are given special markers. There are hundreds of symbols in all. The margins of the map even hint at China and India. The Peutinger Map represents what Romans knew of the world.

The Peutinger Map is written on a parchment scroll and is over 22 feet long (6½ meters)!

Precious Purple

The ancient Phoenicians were amazing sailors. They lived on the eastern end of the Mediterranean Sea in present-day Lebanon, from around 1500 BCE to 300 BCE. Because they stained their skin purple by squeezing a certain type of snail to extract a dye called Tyrian purple, they were known as purple people. Roman emperors and rulers throughout Asia paid a lot of money for this dye. The Phoenicians sailed and traded all around the Mediterranean Sea, and as far as Great Britain. They also sailed south along the coast of Africa, but there are few details and no maps from that time because the Phoenicians kept their knowledge secret from other nations. Along the way, they traded by leaving goods on the shore. If someone wanted their goods, they left an offering for trade next to the goods. If the Phoenicians thought it was a fair trade, they took the payment, and the people knew they could take the goods.

MAKE YOUR OWN

$\mathcal{S}$UNDIAL

1 Look on a globe or map and find the approximate latitude of where you live. Latitudes start at zero at the equator and go to 90 degrees north at the North Pole and 90 degrees south at the South Pole.

2 Set the straight edge of the protractor a half inch (1 centimeter) from the short edge of the paper. Trace around the protractor. Make a dot at the center of the straight edge. Make marks at every 15 degrees around the semicircle and number these as hours as shown here.

3 Make a pinhole through the center dot. Turn the paper over and set the center hole of the protractor on top of the pinhole. Trace around the protractor like before and make marks again every 15 degrees with the hours numbered. You now have two semicircles back-to-back.

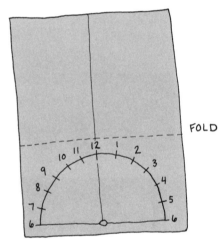

FOLD

4 On one side, draw a line perpendicular to the straight edge of the semicircle, from the pinhole down the length of the paper. Fold the paper about a half inch (1 centimeter) from the edge of the semicircle so this line is on the inside.

5 Push the pencil through the pinhole so it points to the outside of the fold. Set the paper on a table so the eraser end of the pencil is on the table. Position the paper so the pencil is perpendicular to the semicircle and is resting on the line you have drawn. Set your protractor next to the pencil so the center hole of the protractor is in line with where the pencil meets the table.

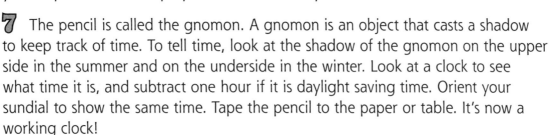

6 Move the pencil along the marked line until the pencil makes the same angle with the table as the degree of longitude where you live. Be sure while you do this that you move the paper so that you keep the semicircle perpendicular with the pencil.

7 The pencil is called the gnomon. A gnomon is an object that casts a shadow to keep track of time. To tell time, look at the shadow of the gnomon on the upper side in the summer and on the underside in the winter. Look at a clock to see what time it is, and subtract one hour if it is daylight saving time. Orient your sundial to show the same time. Tape the pencil to the paper or table. It's now a working clock!

What's Happening?

Shadows change direction depending on the time of day. As the earth rotates and the sun moves across the sky, shadows also move. In the morning, your shadow will stretch out behind you to the west, but in the evening it will stretch to the east. The shadow on your sundial does the same thing.

This type of sundial is called an equatorial sundial because the face of the sundial (the semicircle) is parallel to the equator. The gnomon is parallel to the imaginary axis that the earth spins around. The position of shadows also changes somewhat depending on latitude, which is why the face of your sundial has to be positioned for the latitude where you live. If you live at the equator, your latitude is zero, and the sundial would be perpendicular to the ground and exactly parallel to the equator. If you were at the North Pole, the pencil would be exactly vertical.

The position of shadows also changes somewhat with seasons. Your clock will be most accurate if you orient it on April 15, June 10, September 1, or December 20.

ACTIVITY

MAKE YOUR OWN
Wet Compass

SUPPLIES

* ❋ shallow plastic container, such as one used at a deli
* ❋ water
* ❋ small plastic lid from a juice or milk bottle
* ❋ steel needle
* ❋ bar magnet

1 Fill the plastic container with water to almost full. Gently place the plastic lid in the water with the smooth side down.

2 Hold the needle by the eye. With the other hand, slide the bar magnet along the needle in one direction only, starting at the eye and continuing to the point. Do this about 50 times. Test the needle by placing it near a paper clip. If the paper clip doesn't move, slide the magnet along the needle some more.

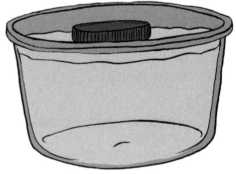

3 Carefully lay the needle across the plastic lid. Make sure any metal objects are put away. Does the plastic lid slowly turn? Let it settle down. One end of the needle should point to north. Check it by using another compass, or by looking on a map of your neighborhood to see which way is north.

What's Happening?

You made the needle become a weak magnet by rubbing another magnet against it. As it floats suspended over the water, it moves to point to magnetic north. For most parts of the United States, magnetic north is not too far off from true north. Which state do you think would have a big difference between magnetic north and true north? **Hint:** Which state is farthest north?

↗ CHAPTER 2 ↖

Explorers Cross the Seas

By the early fifteenth century, many European rulers wanted to encourage **trade** between countries. The rulers needed reliable maps to make sure that traders could travel back and forth between countries by the most direct route. This set off an exciting time in Europe called the **Age of Exploration**.

W**O**rds**2**Know

trade: the exchange of goods for other goods or money.

Age of Exploration: a period from the early 1400s to the early 1600s when Europeans explored and mapped the world.

WOrds2Know

nautical: relating to ships, shipping, sailors, or navigation on a body of water.

nautical chart: a visual representation of an ocean area and the nearby coastal regions.

Europeans already had many of the tools and techniques of the ancient Chinese, Egyptians, Greeks, and Romans, but they weren't enough. Christopher Columbus, for example, used a compass and an astrolabe to help him cross the Atlantic Ocean, but he didn't know his exact position on earth. He thought he had landed in the East Indies (India), when he was really on a Caribbean island over 9,000 miles away from India (14,000 kilometers)! The same was true about maps. There were some accurate maps for smaller areas, but maps of larger areas like oceans couldn't be trusted.

As explorers and navigators set off into unmapped regions, they needed new tools.

New Tools for a New Age

To sail across the Atlantic Ocean and other large bodies of water, sailors needed new maps. A **nautical** map is more commonly called a **nautical chart** and is similar to a road map. Just as land-based topographic maps show features of the land, topographic nautical maps show features in the ocean, like coastlines and islands.

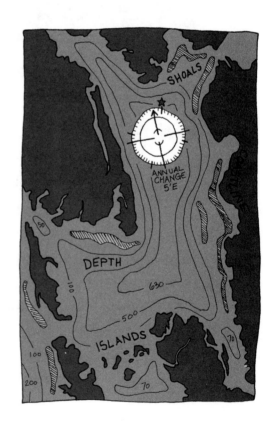

DID YOU KNOW?

To measure the depth of the ocean near the shore, early sailors used **sounding lines**. These are long knotted ropes with weights on the end. Sailors tossed the weights to the ocean floor and counted how many knots went below water.

What's more important though, is that nautical maps contain information about the depth of the water. Some of the most dangerous places for sailing ships are coastlines, where **shoals** can easily cause shipwrecks. Knowing where shoals are can mean the difference between life and death.

The Mercator Projection

As explorers covered larger areas, they ran into the problem of globes vs. maps. Because the earth is a **sphere**, only a globe can accurately represent the real shape of the earth. But a detailed globe would not fit in the ship's cabin. A map could be folded up to fit into a sailor's pocket. And sailors couldn't place a compass on a globe and then steer a straight line in that direction. They would end up spinning slowly off course because of the curve of the globe.

Gerardus Mercator, a cartographer from what is now Belgium, spent his life devoted to mapmaking. He was committed to finding a way to draw the round earth onto a sailor's flat map. Mercator wanted sailors to be able to draw a straight line on a map and keep the same course for the whole voyage.

Words 2 Know

sounding line: a weighted rope used to measure sea depths.

shoal: an area of shallow water.

sphere: a round, three-dimensional object shaped like a ball.

To make his map, Mercator flattened out all lines of longitude. Lines of longitude on a globe are like sections of an orange that come together at the poles. Mercator treated these sections as if they were made out of stretchy elastic and laid them out flat on a map.

No one knows his exact method, but Mercator knew that the sections had to get wider the farther away they got from the equator. He made an even grid out of parallel lines of latitude and longitude.

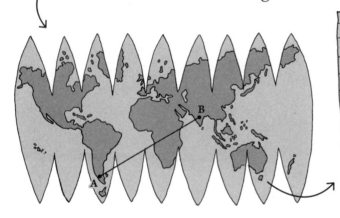

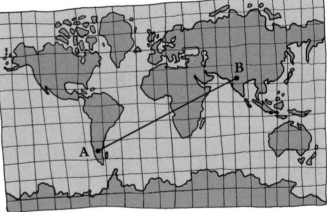

Then, by drawing a **rhumb line** from Point A to Point B, a sailor could set his compass along the line and follow it. A rhumb line crosses all lines of longitude at the same angle. On a globe, rhumb lines are curved. Mercator's map made it so that rhumb lines were straight. His new map, called the **Mercator projection**, came out in 1569 and is still used today.

While the Mercator projection made it easy for sailors to sail straight, it **distorts** the size and shape of seas and land masses. On Mercator's map, Greenland looks almost as large as South America! But South America is actually nine times larger than Greenland. Greenland appears so large because it is so far from the equator, and Mercator's map had to enlarge areas far from the equator in order to keep the rhumb lines straight.

W🔴rds2Know

distort: to make something look different from its normal shape.

map projection: a flat map that represents the globe.

conformal map: a map that preserves the angles between locations.

equal-area map: a map that preserves the area relationships between locations.

→ Map Projections ↰

A **map projection** is any method that represents the surface of a sphere on a flat surface. Every projection distorts the surface in some way. Some distort the scale, while others distort shape or direction. There are dozens of types of projections that serve different purposes. The Mercator projection was a type of **conformal map**, which shows the true shape of small areas but often distorts larger land masses. But any line connecting two points on the map is the same direction a compass would show, so sailors preferred it.

Another type of projection is an **equal-area map**, which shows a mile in Greenland, for example, looking the same as a mile in South America. But the shape of areas and direction are distorted on equal-area maps. Scientists and geographers often prefer equal-area maps because they are more interested in what is occurring on a given land mass than in traveling between them.

DID YOU KNOW?

The highest price ever paid for a map was $10 million in 2003. The Library of Congress bought the 1507 Waldseemüller map, which was the first map to name the U.S. region "America." It is on display in the Library of Congress in Washington, D.C. It's kept in a special case to prevent the map from deteriorating.

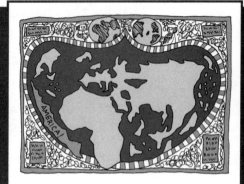

Latitude and Longitude

While sounding lines could measure the distance to the **ocean floor**, navigators still struggled to determine exactly where they were. It was possible to determine latitude—that is, how far north or south of the equator they were. They used the astrolabe to figure that out based on where the sun was at noon or where the North Star was at night, along with what day of the year it was. In 1509, the Portuguese published a 24-page pamphlet giving detailed instructions on how to calculate latitude and a list of latitudes of known places.

ocean floor: the bottom of the ocean.

dead reckoning: a method of determining a ship's position by using a previously determined position and the distance traveled.

But longitude—how far east or west they were—was a different story. Many of the problems faced in making early land maps, like how to measure the distance between two places and how to tell direction, were much more difficult on the water. Sailors used **dead reckoning** to give an estimate of where they were.

28

Dead Reckoning

To use dead reckoning, a sailor determined his location by measuring his course (direction) and the distance traveled from a known point. The course was measured by a magnetic compass. The distance was determined by multiplying the speed of the ship by the time it took to get from one position to another. To figure out the ship's speed, the sailors tossed overboard a small weighted board attached to a line. The board stayed in place as the ship moved forward.

The line had knots at regular intervals and rolled off a reel. They kept track of the time using a sand glass. When the glass ran out of sand, they brought in the board and counted the number of knots that had passed over the side during that time. They could then calculate the speed at which the ship was traveling.

TRY THIS! Why do you think sailors had to know what day of the year it was to calculate their latitude based on the position of the sun or North Star? **Hint:** How does the position of the sun in the sky change between winter and summer?

WOrds2Know

current: the steady flow of water in one direction.

Typically, navigators started dead reckoning from a home port, and they would put a pin in the map to mark the new position at the end of the day. This became the starting position for the next day. The problem is that if you make a small error in figuring out how far you travel, that error gets multiplied over many days. Errors could come in measuring the speed of the ship, or from **currents** or storms pushing the ship off course.

Dead reckoning worked well for short voyages, but over long distances, ships sailed off course without knowing their correct position.

The problem was time. Sailors could determine their longitude if they knew the exact time on the ship and the exact time at the port from where the ship had set sail. This is because longitude is related to time and the rotation of the earth. Every day (24 hours), the earth makes one complete rotation through 360 degrees of a circle. In one hour, the earth rotates through 15 degrees.

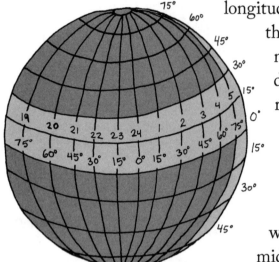

So if you know there is exactly one hour of difference between where you started and where you are now, you know you have traveled 15 degrees. If it were exactly noon on the ship, and exactly midnight at your home port, you would know that you had traveled 180 degrees and that you were exactly halfway around the world from home.

Telling time on the ship was easy at noon each day because the sun would be at its highest point. But how would you know what time it was back home? If you had an accurate clock that was set to the time at the home port, you would know. But even on land, clocks weren't particularly accurate in the 1500s, and at sea they were even less accurate. Most clocks used **pendulums** to mark the time. Have you seen a grandfather clock? This kind of clock uses a pendulum.

But on a boat at sea, that pendulum would get thrown every which way. It would lose track of time.

WOrds2Know

pendulum: a weight hung from a fixed point that swings back and forth.

By the 1700s, determining longitude at sea was still largely a challenge because clocks weren't accurate. It was a huge problem, and many people thought it would never be solved. So in 1714, Britain announced a prize of 20,000 pounds for anyone who could figure out a better method for telling time at sea. To win the prize, the clock could only gain or lose two minutes all the way from Britain to the West Indies.

John Harrison, a carpenter and clockmaker, took up the challenge. He invented the **marine chronometer**, which used a coil spring instead of a pendulum. The spring was not affected by shifts in position like a pendulum was. The clock kept ticking no matter how much a ship tossed and turned. His chronometer even worked upside-down. It lost only a second or two per month and was able to show the correct longitude by keeping track of the time.

It took Harrison four clocks and almost 50 years to develop the clock that met the requirements. British officials finally awarded him the prize in 1773.

WOrds2Know

marine chronometer:
a spring-loaded clock able to keep very precise time at sea.

tick tick tick tick

DID YOU KNOW?

The 20,000 pounds that Britain offered as a prize to develop an accurate marine clock would be equal to about $12 million today!

Captain John Cook was the first explorer to put the marine chronometer to a real test. The British explorer made three separate voyages from Britain to the Pacific Ocean with a marine chronometer on board. He mapped Tahiti, Australia, and New Zealand, all of which were previously known about but not mapped. His maps of these regions were so accurate that they were still used in the mid-twentieth century.

DID YOU KNOW?

When Cook explored the Pacific Islands, he encountered local people who were amazing sailors. They had sailed across the Pacific from south Asia as far as Hawaii in open boats. These Pacific Islanders had established trade routes and charted the waters. They navigated by memorizing the positions of the stars and understanding the patterns of ocean currents and winds.

Shooting the Sun

Words 2 Know

sextant: a navigational instrument used to measure the angle between two objects, usually the horizon and a celestial body.

Another prominent invention was the **sextant**. Whereas an astrolabe measures the angle between one visible object and the zenith, the point directly overhead, a sextant measures the angle between any two visible objects. This is more accurate. A sextant looks like a really complicated tool, but it's quite simple. It's made with an eyepiece, two mirrors, one-sixth of a circle (which is how it gets its name), and a sliding arm.

Matching up two objects tells the angle between them. Normally sailors matched up the sun and the **horizon**, called "shooting the sun." They also used the sextant to measure the angle between two landmarks, which allowed the sailor to calculate the ship's location on a nautical chart.

WOrds2Know

horizon: the line in the distance where the land or sea seems to meet the sky.

Sextants were small and easy to carry aboard ship. They were also extremely accurate. They measured angles to the nearest 10 seconds of a degree, which meant a navigator could place himself within one or two miles of the right position (1.6 to 3.2 kilometers).

Nautical Miles vs. Land Miles

Nautical miles are about 800 feet longer than land miles (244 meters). How did that happen? The mile was originally defined in Roman times as 1,000 paces. The Romans set large stones every thousand paces from Rome to mark the mileage, which is where we get the concept of "milestones." But how do you count paces on the water?

As Ptolemy showed us, the spaces between lines of longitude are greatest at the equator. The equator provides the basis for all nautical miles because it is essentially a circle around the globe. There are 360 degrees in a circle, and each degree can be broken into 60 "minutes." When you divide the circumference of the earth at the equator by how many minutes there are, each minute is a nautical mile. That ends up being 6,076 feet (1,852 meters), which is 796 feet longer than a land mile (243 meters).

360°

1 NAUTICAL MILE

ACTIVITY

MAKE YOUR OWN
MERCATOR PROJECTION

SUPPLIES

* play clay
* large orange
* markers in at least two colors
* table knife
* paper

1 Roll the play clay out to about ¼ inch thick (about ½ centimeter). Drape sections of the clay over the orange until the orange is completely covered. Lay the clay on the orange without pressing hard.

2 With a light-colored marker, draw three circles around the clay that cross like lines of longitude on a globe. With another marker, draw a map on top of the longitude lines. You can draw the continents to make your orange look like the earth, or another design. Make sure that your design covers the whole orange, including the areas near the poles and the equator.

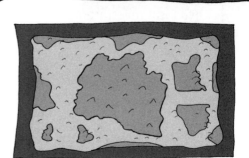

3 Carefully cut along the lines of longitude using the table knife. With your fingers, carefully lift each section of clay off the orange. Lay each section on the paper, lining them up so they touch each other at the equator.

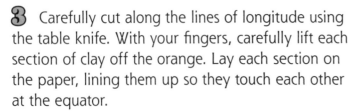

4 Gently stretch the clay with your fingers so that each section becomes a rectangle and the sections form a solid rectangle with no gaps.

What's Happening?

What you have done is like what happens in a Mercator projection. To keep the lines of latitude and longitude parallel, some areas have to be stretched. Stretching from left to right changes the shape of your design. If you wanted to keep the shape the same, how else might you stretch the clay? Look at a Mercator projection. How does the distance between lines of latitude change from the equator to the North and South Poles?

ACTIVITY

SUPPLIES

* paper
* pen or pencil
* world map or globe

PREDICT YOUR
*L*ATITUDE AND *L*ONGITUDE

1 How well do you know the latitude and longitude of where you live? Write down the names of cities or countries around the world that you think are at the same longitude as where you live, which means they would be exactly north or south of where you are. Do the same for cities or countries that are at the same latitude, which means they would be exactly east or west of where you live. Which city or country do you think is on the opposite side of the world from you?

2 Write down the following cities and guess whether they are north or south of where you live and whether they are east or west of where you live.

* London, England
* Madrid, Spain
* Moscow, Russia
* Oslo, Norway
* Mexico City, Mexico
* Sydney, Australia
* Addis Ababa, Ethiopia
* Quito, Ecuador
* Rio de Janeiro, Brazil
* Kathmandu, Nepal

3 Check on a globe to see how close you came. Were there any surprises?

What's Happening?

People often think Europe is farther south than it is because it has relatively warm weather. That's because the Gulf Stream, a large current that flows south to north along the East Coast and then west to east across the Atlantic Ocean, brings warmer water to Europe. It seems like South America would be exactly south of North America, but it isn't. The west coast of South America roughly lines up with the east coast of North America!

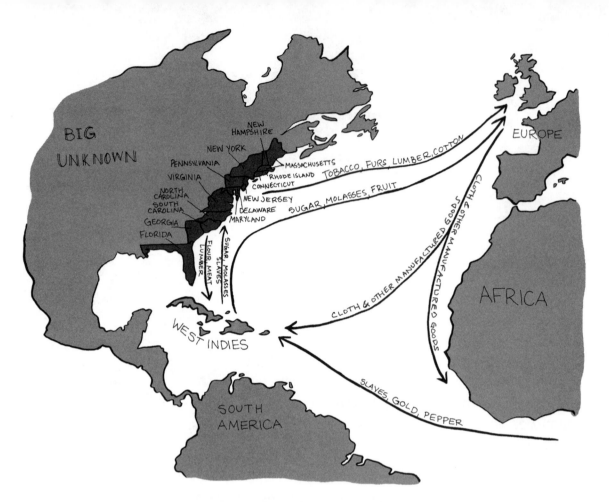

↗ CHAPTER 3 ↖

Mapping New Lands and New Skies

With the Mercator projection and new tools like the sextant and marine chronometer, explorers could cross the seas more easily. Why was it important to map their voyages accurately? So that others could follow behind them and arrive at the same place. But for the Europeans, the **New World** was uncharted territory. As settlements grew in new corners of the world, new maps were needed.

Lewis and Clark

Governments across the world have a history of providing money for navigation and mapping. European kings and rulers paid for explorers to open up trade routes. By 1800, the United States was an independent country and its eastern shore was settled. Thomas Jefferson, its third president, wanted to open the western wilderness for trade and settlement.

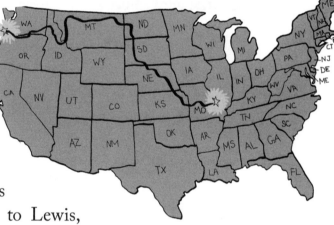

WOrds2Know

New World: North and South America.

terrain: the physical features of land.

President Jefferson especially wanted to find a water route to the Pacific Ocean. He selected U.S. Army Captain Meriwether Lewis to lead what was known as the Corps of Discovery. In his 1803 letter to Lewis, Jefferson wrote: "Beginning at the mouth of the Missouri, you will take careful observations of latitude & longitude, at all remarkable points on the river. The variations of the compass too, in different places, should be noticed."

Lewis selected William Clark as his partner for the voyage. Jefferson supplied the expedition with everything Lewis and Clark would need on their journey. Surviving would be hard, let alone obeying the orders of a president who wanted "careful observations." Lewis and Clark expected to find dangerous animals and difficult **terrain**. No one knew how far the Missouri River reached, and they had only rough maps of the areas.

Lewis and Clark set out by boat down the Ohio River. Over the 28 months of their journey, they made daily measurements of latitude and longitude. Lewis and Clark often stood on one bluff and pointed at another, marking it as their new destination. They relied on their compass to chart the direction they'd be traveling. Their chronometer tracked how long it took them to reach the new bluff.

Lewis and Clark made detailed notes on their travels.

They described 122 animals and 178 plants that had never before been written about in the history of science. Think of all the plants, animals, and insects you walk past on a daily basis, but probably don't notice. Lewis and Clark were careful observers of life on earth, taking great care not to walk right past anything. They serve as a reminder that while great navigators must be bold, they must also be careful and detailed observers.

WOrds 2 Know

surveyor: someone who measures land areas to set up boundaries.

DID YOU KNOW?

Thomas Jefferson was the son of a **surveyor**. Before George Washington was president of the United States, he was also a surveyor.

Sacagawea

President Jefferson wanted Lewis and Clark to establish good relationships with the Native Americans they met. Sacagawea was a member of the Shoshone tribe who went on the Corps of Discovery expedition with her husband. She served as an **interpreter** for Lewis and Clark and was able to help them trade with local tribes for food and horses during their long trip. When the expedition struggled to find food crossing the **Continental Divide**, she showed them how to dig roots and eat certain types of bark for nourishment. Amazingly, she was pregnant during much of the trip, which turned out to be to the advantage of the expedition. When Lewis and Clark encountered Native American tribes on their travels, the people were put at ease by the sight of a pregnant woman traveling with the expedition. Dozens of land features have been named for Sacagawea, and many memorials and films have been created in her honor.

Lewis and Clark didn't find a new water route to the Pacific Ocean because there wasn't one.

They had to cross the Rocky Mountains on foot. But they did publish a map in 1814 with distances and locations accurate to within 5 percent. This was considered an enormous achievement at the time. Maps of the region wouldn't be improved upon for nearly 100 years, until **aerial** maps could be made.

WOrds2Know

interpreter: someone who translates from one language to another.

Continental Divide: a ridge of mountains running from northwestern Canada through Mexico that separates the waters that flow into the Atlantic Ocean or Gulf of Mexico from those that flow into the Pacific Ocean.

aerial: relating to the air.

Surveyors

Surveyors determined distances and areas of land, as well as elevations. This was an important job in **Colonial America** because property had to be legally divided. Surveyors used chains of a specific length to measure distance. They staked one end of the chain into the ground and used a compass to extend the chain along a straight line in a specific direction. The first stake was then brought up to where the second one was and the process started over.

Mountains and Canyons

Can you imagine the challenges faced by explorers like Lewis and Clark? Explorers encountered many difficult mountain ranges: the Appalachian Mountains in the eastern United States, the Adirondack Mountains in upstate New York, and the Rocky Mountains out west. High mountains could be difficult barriers to get past. Weather was unpredictable and difficult, climbing was dangerous, and breathing was more difficult at high **altitudes**. Explorers had to figure out the best way through the mountains. To do that, they had to map mountains from a distance.

W**O**rds**2**Know

Colonial America: the name given to America when talking about the years 1607–1776 when new settlers came from Europe and before the United States became its own country.

altitude: the height of something above the level of the sea. Also called elevation.

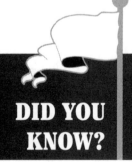

DID YOU KNOW?

A medical condition called altitude sickness can occur at high elevation in the mountains. This is because the air at high altitudes contains less oxygen than the air at sea level. Too little oxygen in the blood makes a person feel light-headed, tired, and nauseous.

WOrds2Know

triangulation: the process of determining location and distance to a point by measuring the angles of a fixed baseline of known length.

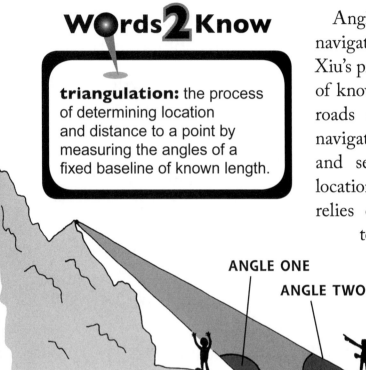

ANGLE ONE

ANGLE TWO

DISTANCE

Angles have been important to navigators throughout history. Pei Xiu's principles stated the importance of knowing the angles and curves of roads and natural features. Many navigational tools like the astrolabe and sextant use angles to project location. The Mercator projection relies on keeping angles the same to find a straight route from place to place.

Mapping mountains also required the use of angles in a method called **triangulation**.

If you know the distance between two locations, and the angle from each of these locations to a third location, you can figure out the rest of the distances and angles in that triangle. Explorers used triangulation to measure unknown distances to places that were difficult to reach, like mountaintops.

For a long time, canyons were just blank spots on maps. No one wanted to risk the dangers of exploring their depths, so they were just left empty on maps. The Grand Canyon is a good example of one such blank spot. For thousands or perhaps even millions of years, the Colorado River had cut through the earth, eventually producing a canyon so "grand" that it was over 1 mile deep (1.6 kilometers), 10 miles wide (16 kilometers), and almost 300 miles long (483 kilometers).

WOrds 2 Know

barometer: a scientific instrument used to measure air pressure.

atmospheric pressure: the amount of force pressing down on you by the weight of the air.

mercury: a liquid metal used inside thermometers.

People thought the Grand Canyon was impossible to map.

In 1869, John Wesley Powell led an expedition of 10 men on what is now known as the Colorado River Exploring Expedition. Over 99 days, they traveled 1,000 miles on the dangerous, uncharted Colorado River that cut through the Grand Canyon (1,600 kilometers). The cliffs were often too steep for them to pull out their boats or make camp. They always feared a waterfall might be right around the bend. They took along chronometers, compasses, and sextants to map the canyon.

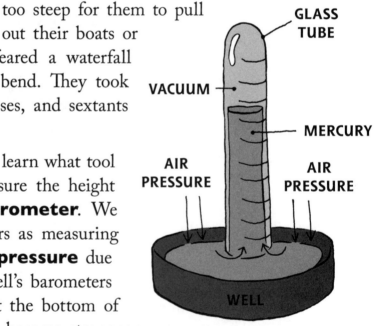

You might be surprised to learn what tool the expedition used to measure the height of the canyon walls. A **barometer**. We normally think of barometers as measuring changes in **atmospheric pressure** due to changes in weather. Powell's barometers held a well of **mercury** at the bottom of a glass tube. As air pressure became stronger, more mercury would rise up the glass tube. When the pressure lessened, some of the mercury would go back down to the well at the bottom.

Barometers can measure altitude because atmospheric pressure drops as altitude rises.

One man stayed at the bottom of the canyon to take readings on a barometer. Meanwhile, Powell and another man climbed the canyon walls and took readings on another barometer of the pressure from different heights. By comparing the readings on the two barometers, they could determine the change in altitude. They did this all along the Colorado River to help determine both the height of the canyon walls and changes in elevation at the bottom of the canyon.

TRY THIS!

Powell could have used just one barometer and taken readings at the bottom then later farther up the canyon. Why do you think Powell wanted someone to stay at the bottom of the canyon to take readings at the same time that he took them higher up the canyon walls? What might happen to the barometric readings if a storm rolled in while they were taking readings?

John Wesley Powell

John Wesley Powell was a bold man who lived a fascinating life and accomplished impressive feats even before his expeditions to the West. In his twenties he spent four months walking across Wisconsin, rowed down the Mississippi River to the sea, and rowed from Pittsburgh to St. Louis on the Ohio River. He also fought in the Civil War for the Union, losing an arm in the Battle of Shiloh. Powell was a professor of **geology** at Illinois State and Illinois Wesleyan University.

After his adventures, he was named the second director of the U.S. Geological Survey (USGS) and Director of Ethnology at the Smithsonian Institution. In 1884, John Wesley Powell asked the U.S. Congress to authorize the USGS to begin systematically making topographic maps of the United States.

WOrds2Know

geology: the scientific study of the history and physical nature of the earth.

Flight: Mapping Takes Off!

Have you ever been on a plane waiting for it to take off and heard the pilot say he was "waiting for clearance"? Maybe you've seen the tall control tower that sits high above the other buildings at an airport. Air traffic controllers help keep track of different planes in the air to make sure there is plenty of space for everyone. When driving cars, we have roads and traffic signs to keep us organized. But up in the sky, much like at sea, navigation can be trickier.

WOrds2Know

aeronautical chart: a map designed to assist in the navigation of an airplane.

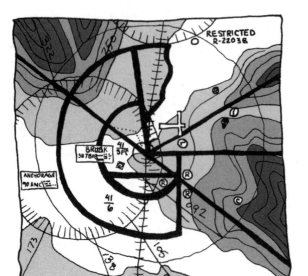

No matter where you travel, you need maps. **Aeronautical charts** show pilots where to fly an aircraft the same way roadmaps help drivers. They show things like the safest routes, landmarks to look out for, and landing fields.

As planes improved throughout the twentieth century, they became capable of longer flights. Pilots covered more miles than any explorers before them. They didn't have time to make the slow and careful calculations with sextants and astrolabes because they needed to focus on flying. How did they navigate?

The simplest is visual navigation. Under the right weather conditions and in certain areas, pilots can find their way using their own eyes and aeronautical charts. To know where they are, pilots compare what is on the maps with what they see. In the early years of flight navigation, pilots used visual navigation and generally flew from city to city.

WOrds2Know

But visual navigation doesn't work at night or in bad weather.

beacon: a fire or light set in a visible location as a warning or signal.

Pilots also needed the help of instruments. The first navigational aid developed for flight was a **beacon** that rotated in a full circle and looked as if it were flashing. Beacons were first used in the 1920s along regular routes to help pilots fly at night. They were limited though. What if the weather was overcast and the pilot couldn't see the beacons? What if a plane was blown far off course? What about in the daytime? Beacons wouldn't show objects that might be in your way, and they couldn't be used to cross the ocean!

Amelia Earhart

Amelia Earhart became an international icon during her courageous aviation career. Her life was full of daring adventures and exploration, and included many aviation "firsts."

✸ **1928:** first woman to cross the Atlantic Ocean by airplane.

✸ **1932:** first woman and second person ever to fly solo across the Atlantic Ocean.

✸ **1935:** first person to fly solo between California and Hawaii.

✸ **1935:** first woman to compete in the National Air Races in Cleveland.

In 1937, Earhart attempted to fly around the world along the equator—the longest round-the-world flight at the time. Her plane disappeared over the Pacific Ocean during the final legs of the flight. A search has been going on ever since.

Radio Navigation

Pilots needed more than blinking lights and visual maps to fly safely around the world. **Radio waves** came to the rescue. Through **radio navigation**, pilots sent and received **Morse Code** signals that gave them information about where they were and what was around them. Have you ever used navigation on a smartphone? It relies on signals from satellites.

Early radio navigation didn't have satellites, it was all ground based. An **antenna** at a station on the ground transmitted a signal to a pilot using radio waves. Knowing the location of the station and the direction of the signal, a pilot could determine the location of their plane.

WOrds2Know

radio wave: an electromagnetic wave used to transmit radio and television signals and for navigation.

radio navigation: the use of radio frequencies to determine one's position on the earth and navigate a ship or airplane.

Morse Code: an alphabet represented by combinations of long and short signals.

antenna: a metal rod that sends and receives radio waves.

Today, with the availability of satellites, pilots use a variety of sophisticated and accurate radio navigation systems to fly safely.

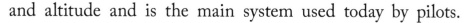

GPS: Global Positioning System (GPS) is a system that transmits information through radio waves from a network of satellites. It tells pilots exactly where they are in latitude, longitude, and altitude and is the main system used today by pilots.

VOR: Very High Frequency Omnidirectional Range navigation system (VOR) provides a bearing, or direction, for the plane. VOR has been widely used since the 1950s and is still used today as a backup to GPS. There are about 3,000 VHF (Very High Frequency) stations around the world, and planes are built to receive signals from all of them.

Pilots can check an aeronautical chart to see which frequencies they are flying toward and set their navigation equipment to receive a certain signal. A needle on the navigation equipment tells the pilot if he or she is headed toward the signal. The pilot can then make adjustments.

DME: Distance Measuring Equipment (DME) measures a plane's distance from several fixed points. It uses pairs of radio pulses sent and received by ground stations. Like VOR, it is used today as a backup to GPS.

Another Way to Tell Where You Are

Inertial navigation systems use computers and motion-detecting devices to determine where a plane is positioned at all times. These systems work a lot like the dead reckoning that ancient sailors used, but with very accurate ways of measuring distance traveled and direction.

An inertial navigation system first gets its position from somewhere else (like a person or GPS), and then uses an **accelerometer** and **gyroscope** to calculate its position as it changes. The accelerometer measures the plane's changes in speed. A gyroscope measures changes in direction.

W O rds 2 Know

accelerometer: a device used to measures acceleration.

gyroscope: a spinning wheel or disk used to measure or maintain orientation.

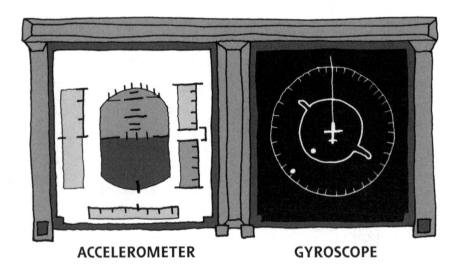

ACCELEROMETER   GYROSCOPE

Gyroscopes are like tops or wheels that never stop spinning and are always detecting shifts in direction.

Imagine sitting in the passenger's seat of a car wearing a blindfold. Would you be able to tell when the car goes up a large hill? You would probably feel yourself leaning back in your seat. If the car took a hard left turn, your shoulder might bump into the door. These are the types of changes that an inertial navigation system tracks. It constantly tracks changes in speed and direction and always knows exactly where a plane is and where it's going. This same technology is used to help space shuttles, missiles, and submarines guide themselves.

DID YOU KNOW?

The first flight to carry airmail across the United States was in 1921. The Post Office lit bonfires to show the way.

Wild Imaginations and Outright Fakes!

Many times, when mapmakers didn't know what was in an area, they filled it in with what they thought should be there. For example, for almost all of the 1800s, maps of Africa showed the Kong Mountains stretching from the west coast of Africa into the interior of the continent. Look on a modern map or globe and see if you can find the Kong Mountains anywhere.

Sometimes, mapmakers or explorers were more devious. Benjamin Morrell, an explorer of the Southern Hemisphere in the early 1800s, mapped at least 123 fake islands. He named one "imaginary" island near Hawaii after himself. It wasn't until about 1917 that the last of the fake islands was removed from official maps!

1800s
(Kong Mountains)

MODERN DAY
(no Kong Mountains)

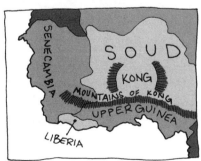

Radar: What's Around You

To navigate safely, you have to know what's around you. Planes use **radar** devices that send out radio signals through an antenna to help pilots see what obstacles are around them. When a signal reaches an object, it bounces back to a scanner on the plane. The scanner calculates the distance to the object from the time it took the signal to return to the plane.

Think of it like tossing a ball against a wall. When you stand close to a wall and toss a ball against it, the ball bounces back to you quickly. But from farther away, it takes longer to travel to the wall and also longer to get back to you. Air traffic controllers also use radar to detect other aircraft and to guide them to land in bad weather with poor visibility.

W**O**rds**2**Know

radar: a system for detecting the presence of aircraft or other objects. It uses radio waves reflected from surfaces.

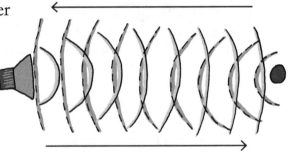

RETURN SIGNAL FROM OBJECT

SIGNAL FROM PLANE

Aerial Photography

With powered flight, it wasn't long before people began taking pictures of the earth from airplanes. This allowed for much faster and more accurate mapmaking. Aerial photographs used for mapmaking are taken with a special camera attached to the bottom of an airplane. The photographs overlap each other to make sure all details are captured. Today, the USGS regularly takes aerial photographs from both airplanes and satellites to make topographic maps, to map geology and mineral resources, and to evaluate floodplains. Scientists also use them to understand changes on the surface of the earth over time.

ACTIVITY

MAKE YOUR OWN
*C*ONTOUR *M*AP

1 Shape a mountain from clay a few inches high and put it into the bowl (7½ centimeters). Cut some areas of clay out of the mountain to give it an irregular shape. Make one side of the mountain have a steep slope and the other side have a gradual slope. Tape the ruler along the side of the bowl so the zero mark is even with the bottom of the bowl.

2 Add water to the bowl up to the ½-inch mark on the ruler (6.3 millimeters). Press the string into the clay, circling the mountain along the line that the water hits the clay.

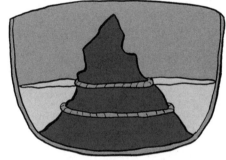

SIDE VIEW

3 Repeat step 2, adding ½ inch of water each time (6.3 millimeters), until the water covers all of the clay. You should have several lines of string that encircle your mountain and are parallel to each other.

4 Look at your mountain from straight above and draw a picture on your paper showing the strings as they appear from above. Color the areas between the lines with different colors. You might try using different shades, with darker shades at the bottom of the mountain and lighter shades near the top.

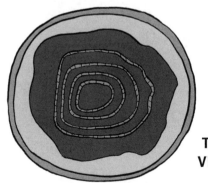

TOP VIEW

What's Happening?

The lines that you have drawn to represent the string are contour lines. Contours are imaginary lines that join places of the same height. When they're close together, it means the land is steep. When they're far apart, it means the land is gentle or flat.

ACTIVITY

SUPPLIES

* 3 brightly colored objects that can rest on the ground without moving
* measuring tape at least 10 feet long (3 meters)
* several sheets of 8½ by 11 inch paper (210 x 296 millimeters)
* clear tape
* pencil
* ruler
* protractor with an arm
* large book

DO YOUR OWN

*T*RIANGULATION

1 Find a flat, empty place that is at least 10 feet by 20 feet in area (3 by 6 meters). On one end, place one of the objects on the ground. This is your point A. Using the measuring tape, place the second object exactly 10 feet away (3 meters). This is your point B and the imaginary line between them is your baseline. Leave the measuring tape in place.

2 Tape at least two sheets of paper together along the long side. Use the ruler to draw a baseline 10 inches long (25 centimeters). It should be parallel to the taped side and about ½ inch away from the edge (just over 1 centimeter). Mark one end point A and the other end point B. This baseline represents the baseline between the two objects on the ground. Your scale is 1 inch (25.4 millimeters) = 1 foot (30.5 centimeters), which means that 1 inch on your paper is the same as 1 foot on the ground.

3 Place the third object on the ground so that the three objects form a triangle. This third object is point C. Don't measure the distance yet, but use your eyes to make it a little farther away from either point A or B than they are from each other.

4 Use the protractor to measure the angle at point A between your baseline and point C. Place the zero line of the protractor along the baseline with the circle or open hole of the protractor at point A. Get down close to the protractor at the circle or open hole of the protractor and move the arm so it's pointed toward point C. Write down the angle.

52

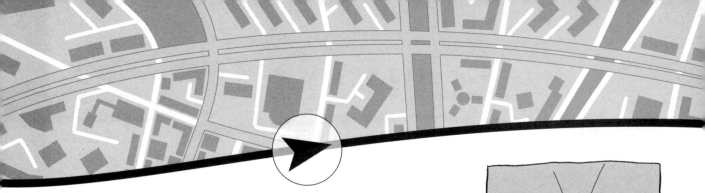

5 Without moving the arm of the protractor, place it on point A on your paper and make a mark where the arm is. Use your ruler to draw a line from point A through your mark and as long as possible without going off the page.

6 Repeat steps 4 and 5, measuring the angle from point B. The two lines that you drew from points A and B should cross. Mark the intersection point C. If the lines run off the paper before crossing, attach another piece of paper.

7 Measure the two lines from points A to C and points B to C to the nearest ¼ inch (6.3 millimeters). Write them down next to the lines. However many inches the lines are, the distance on the ground should be the same in feet. Measure the distances between the objects from points A to C and B to C. Are they similar to what you predicted from measuring on paper? What might account for any differences?

What's Happening?

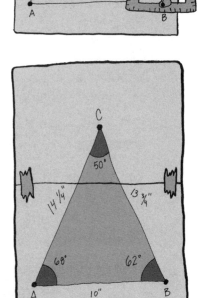

You might have seen a difference between the distances you predicted from the map measurements and the actual measurements. A tiny error on the map makes a larger error in life. Surveyors measure much larger distances, so they have to use very accurate instruments. To quickly and accurately calculate distances, they also use a branch of mathematics called trigonometry, which deals with triangles and the relationships between their sides and angles. This is even more important when there are changes in elevation, because that affects the distances.

ACTIVITY

MAKE YOUR OWN
*B*ACKYARD *M*AP

SUPPLIES

* ✳ paper
* ✳ colored pencils
* ✳ notebook

1 Draw a map of your backyard, noting trees, shrubs, areas of grass, areas of flowers or vegetables, and any big rocks or steep slopes. Mark any objects made by humans, such as a rock wall, fence, garden, sandbox, or swing.

2 Go to a section of your backyard and map what's there in detail. For example, if you have a garden, you might mark each plant. Put a small 1 in the area on your map.

3 In your notebook, write 1 and make detailed notes about what you see. Are there any insects? What is the soil like? Draw a sketch of a plant or insect if you like.

What's Happening?

You have made an **annotated map**. Were you surprised by what you saw when you looked closely and took your time? These are the types of careful observations that Lewis and Clark made on their journey.

W**O**rds**2**Know

annotated map: a map with descriptions or explanations.

Mapping India

In the 1800s the British used triangulation and extremely careful calculations to map all of India in the Great Trigonometric Survey of India. Mount Everest was named after Sir George Everest, who led the survey. When they measured Mount Everest in 1852 using triangulation, they found it to be 29,002 feet high (8840 meters). Mount Everest was measured using GPS in 1999 and found to be 29,035 feet (8850 meters). That's only 33 feet different (10 meters)!

CHAPTER 4

Mapping from Satellites: GPS and Landsat

Far overhead, there are about 3,000 active, artificial satellites that orbit the earth. They have all been launched by different nations for various purposes. A satellite is any object that moves around a larger object. The moon is a natural satellite around earth. Artificial satellites carry instruments and sensors that collect information and send it back to earth. Some collect information about the weather and atmosphere. Others collect information about planets, navigation, and position, or take pictures of the earth.

From Planes to Satellites

How did we get from using planes to map the earth to using satellites? In the twentieth century, advancements in both flight and radar played a large role in the **politics** of the time. During World War II, the Germans made great advancements in rockets and missiles. They produced what is considered the first modern rocket, called the V-2 rocket, which could travel a distance of 200 miles (322 kilometers).

WOrds2Know

politics: the business of governments.

Space Race: the competition between the United States and the Soviet Union to achieve the greatest accomplishments in space exploration.

coordinates: numbers used to determine the position of a point, line, or surface.

In 1957, the Soviet Union (now Russia) launched Sputnik, the first satellite, into space. By the 1960s, the United States military was trying to outdo the advancements of the Soviet Union in what became known as the **Space Race**. The United States wanted to have its own satellites in space that it could use to direct missiles launched from submarines. The idea was that satellites could beam exact positioning **coordinates** to submarines in the ocean so their aim would be more precise. Since then the United States has launched many more satellites into space for all types of uses.

SPUTNIK

Satellites have transformed the way that we see our planet and how people map and navigate in the air and on the ground. One of the most important developments for mapmaking is the Global Positioning System, or GPS.

GPS

If you've ever been in a car with a device that gives directions to help you get somewhere, you have used or seen GPS. Have your parents asked you to use the GPS while they are driving? All you had to do to navigate was simply put in the address of your destination and follow the map the GPS provided. The device is called a GPS receiver because it receives signals from GPS satellites. GPS is a space-based satellite navigation system that provides time and location information to GPS receivers on earth.

Emperor Penguin Colonies

It's hard to get an accurate count of penguins on Antarctica. Until recently, scientists counted from the ground or used aerial photography. But Antarctica is a large, cold continent. Most of the penguin colonies are in areas that are as cold as -58 degrees Fahrenheit (-50 degrees Celsius) and are difficult or impossible to get to.

high resolution: showing a lot of detail.

Early in 2012, scientists counted emperor penguins using **high-resolution** images from satellites that showed the penguins' shadows and droppings. Scientists have estimated there are almost 600,000 emperor penguins in Antarctica. In late 2012, scientists used the images to find a new colony of 9,000 penguins, with three-quarters of them chicks.

But the sea ice in Antarctica is melting and scientists worry about the penguins. They predict that the Terre Adélie emperor colony in Antarctica will shrink from 3,000 breeding pairs today to between 500 and 600 by the year 2100.

The GPS system is owned and operated by the U.S. government and is free to all users. The system has three parts:

1. A satellite system to transmit signals. The GPS satellites transmit information to earth using radio signals. There are 31 actively **broadcasting** satellites, operated by the United States Air Force. They form what is known as the **GPS constellation**. At least 24 satellites are available at all times. All the satellites travel the same path every day in the exact same orbit. Depending on the time of day, your house has anywhere from 8 to 10 satellites overhead.

Words 2 Know

broadcast: to send out signals to be received by radio or television receivers.

GPS constellation: the movement and relationship of the 31 GPS satellites in space.

solar power: energy from the sun.

atomic clock: an extremely accurate timekeeping device controlled by the vibrations of **atoms**.

atom: the smallest particle of matter in the universe that makes up everything, like tiny building blocks or grains of sand.

DID YOU KNOW?

Every 9 billionths of a second is one tick on an atomic clock.

Each satellite travels about 12,600 miles (20,200 kilometers) above the earth and orbits the planet twice a day. The satellites weigh 3,000 to 4,000 pounds (1,360 to 1,814 kilograms) and use **solar power**. Each has multiple **atomic clocks**, which are the most reliable source of timekeeping in the world.

2. A worldwide system of stations to control the satellites. All of those satellites have to be controlled to make sure they stay on course and are closely tracked. There is an entire command center devoted to tracking these satellites. The GPS master control station is near Colorado Springs, Colorado, located at the Schriever Air Force Base. A network of other monitor stations around the globe constantly tracks and sends commands to the satellites.

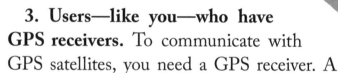

3. Users—like you—who have GPS receivers. To communicate with GPS satellites, you need a GPS receiver. A GPS receiver receives the satellite signal and calculates its position. To calculate the distance between the satellite and the receiver, the receiver compares the time the signal was sent with the time it was received. Just as with the development of the nautical clock, knowing the exact time is the key.

WOrds2Know

trilateration: the process of determining location by measuring distance between known objects.

In a process called **trilateration**, the GPS receiver uses the distance to several satellites to calculate its exact position. Trilateration is a lot like triangulation, but it uses distances instead of angles.

Imagine you're lost somewhere in the United States. You have no idea where you are and you have no navigational devices to help you find your way. You ask a passerby, "Where am I?" She tells you that you're 105 miles from Cincinnati (169 kilometers).

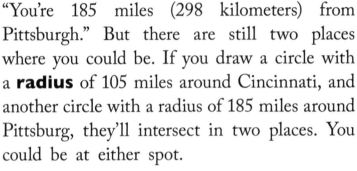

radius: the distance from the center of a circle to every point along the edge of that circle.

But Cincinnati could be 105 miles in any direction. You ask another person where you are and he says "You're 185 miles (298 kilometers) from Pittsburgh." But there are still two places where you could be. If you draw a circle with a **radius** of 105 miles around Cincinnati, and another circle with a radius of 185 miles around Pittsburg, they'll intersect in two places. You could be at either spot.

Finally, you ask a third person, and she says, "You are 140 miles (225 kilometers) from Cleveland." If you then draw a third circle with a 140-mile radius around Cleveland, it will only intersect with one of the other two points that intersected in the first two circles. Then you can be sure: you're in Columbus, Ohio!

GPS works in a similar way. At any given time, GPS satellites transmit radio signals that give the satellite's position and time. A receiver then keeps track of the distances to several satellites, and calculates its position on the earth using trilateration.

What's the Fuss About GPS?

One of the best things about GPS is that it's free and open to the public. This means that anyone with a GPS receiver can use it to figure out where they are. GPS receivers are used on all kinds of devices to help people know their exact position and time, or to track objects. The technology keeps getting better and better. Today, receivers can mark your position to within three feet (1 meter). GPS also provides extremely accurate time, which is critical for many uses.

DID YOU KNOW? The latest satellites launched in May 2010 tell time so well, they are accurate to within eight-billionths of a second per day!

Here are some ways people use GPS every day:

- Navigation for vehicles, trains, and boats
- Cell phones
- Tracking shipping containers and packages
- Airplanes/air traffic control
- Military equipment and vehicles
- On buoys to track the spread of oil spills
- Tracking endangered animals
- Search and rescue of people

Enhanced GPS

There are various systems that add other data to GPS data to make position and time information even more accurate. Some of these systems allow a receiver to be accurate to within centimeters or even millimeters in certain locations.

One such system is the National Geodetic Survey, operated by the U.S. **National Oceanic and Atmospheric Agency (NOAA)**. Have you ever heard of the branch of science called **geodesy**? It focuses on the size and shape of the earth and the location of points on its surface.

A geodesist is a scientist specializing in geodesy.

WOrds2Know

National Oceanic and Atmospheric Agency (NOAA): a United States government agency focused on the condition of the oceans and the atmosphere.

geodesy: the study of the size and shape of the earth and the location of points on its surface.

Stranded in the Indian Ocean

On January 23, 2010, 16-year-old Abby Sunderland set sail in an attempt to become the youngest person to sail solo around the world. On June 10, fierce winds broke the mast on her boat as she was sailing in the middle of the Indian Ocean. She was 2,000 miles (3,219 kilometers) west of Australia, in an area rarely visited by ships. She was alone, with no help in sight.

Fortunately, Abby had special radio beacons with her. Abby activated her beacons, which sent a distress signal. GPS satellites received the signal and computers calculated her position. Within an hour her position was pinpointed. A fishing vessel 400 miles away (645 kilometers) rescued her—safe and in good health.

Geodesists for the National Geodetic Survey have placed about 850,000 survey markers throughout the United States over the past 200 years. These markers have exact coordinates both horizontally and vertically. With GPS, the coordinates can be located to within millimeters, and then tracked over time. Geodesy is used in making accurate maps of large areas of the earth that need to take into account the curvature of the earth's surface.

Scientists also use this precise information in other ways, such as restoring **wetlands** and locating an earthquake's **epicenter**. Wetlands are extremely important to the overall health of **ecosystems**, but they are delicate. They can be affected by a change in elevation of mere millimeters. Having exact elevations as shown by the geodetic markers helps scientists monitor the health of wetlands. It also helps them restore damaged wetlands by selecting the best vegetation to use in replanting.

WOrds2Know

wetland: an area where the land is soaked with water, such as a swamp.

epicenter: the point on the earth's surface directly above the location of an earthquake.

ecosystem: a community of plants and animals living in the same area and relying on each other to survive.

Words2Know

plate tectonics: the scientific **theory** that describes the large-scale movement of the plates in the earth's crust.

theory: an idea or set of ideas intended to explain something.

geologist: a scientist who studies the solid and liquid matter that make up the earth and the forces that shape it.

Landsat: a satellite system operated by the U.S. government that studies and photographs the earth's surface.

Changes in location are also especially important when it comes to **plate tectonics**. When the earth's plates are moving, it's time to watch for volcanic eruptions and earthquakes. Because these plates can be as large as an entire continent and their movement is slow, it is nearly impossible for the human eye to track them.

Enhanced GPS networks help geodesists and **geologists** locate the position of tectonic plates to within millimeters and track their changing position over time.

With this information, researchers can quickly locate an earthquake's epicenter.

GPS
12,600 miles

LANDSAT
438 miles

Landsat: Pictures from Space

The **Landsat** program is another important development in mapmaking. In July 1972, the United States launched the first Landsat, a satellite that now surveys earth from 438 miles above the surface (705 kilometers). Landsat's pictures of earth's forests, rivers, oceans, glaciers, crops, and cities have transformed mapping and our view of the physical world.

There are two Landsat satellites orbiting the North and South Poles. One passes overhead every 18 days, continuously taking pictures.

64

Each satellite has a mirror that scans back and forth. Light from the ground reflects off the mirror into a **telescope** and is focused into light detectors. The detectors sense not only visible light, but also light that people can't see, like **infrared light**. We feel infrared light as heat, which means that Landsat images show how much heat is **radiating** from an area.

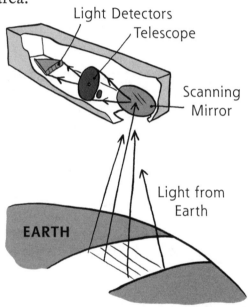

Light Detectors
Telescope
Scanning Mirror
Light from Earth
EARTH

WOrds2Know

telescope: a tool used to see objects that are far away.

infrared light: **radiation** that has longer wavelengths than visible light, and can be felt as heat by humans.

radiation: energy transmitted in the form of rays, waves, or particles from a source, such as the sun.

radiate: to spread outward.

environmental: relating to the natural world and the impact of human activity on its condition.

All of the Landsat data is free and available to the public.

Tracking changes in population and the land over time is valuable to all kinds of researchers, especially those who deal with **environmental** issues. Experts in agriculture, forestry, land use, water resources, and natural resource exploration all depend on Landsat images. Just imagine how helpful these photographs can be to identify crop types and predict harvest times, find archaeological sites, locate new oil reserves, track climate change and population growth, and manage fires and forests.

Using Landsat to Track Water Use

In many parts of the world, water is **scarce** and needs to be carefully monitored. In most areas, farmers are the biggest users of water. But it can be difficult to measure just how much water an individual farm is using. Researchers use Landsat images to help calculate water use so farmers can keep improving how they **irrigate** their crops and how they can **conserve** and reuse water.

WOrds2Know

scarce: in short supply.

irrigate: to supply land with water, usually for crops.

conserve: to use something carefully, so it doesn't get used up.

evaporation: the process of a liquid heating up and changing into a gas, such as water vapor.

transpiration: the process by which a plant pulls water up through its roots, which then collects on its leaves and evaporates into the atmosphere.

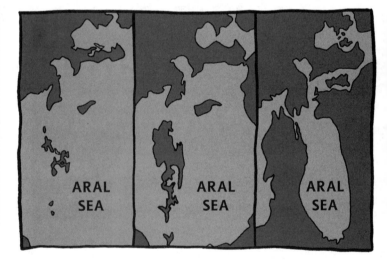

1977   1989   2006

ARAL SEA   ARAL SEA   ARAL SEA

Landsat imagery of the shrinking sea

Landsat takes images that are 30 meters square—about the size of a baseball diamond. The images are the perfect size for pictures of fields of crops. Landsat measures the amount of solar energy that goes into heating the ground and air and the **evaporation** of water from an area and **transpiration** from plants. It then uses the measurements to accurately measure water use by farmers and other users.

ACTIVITY

MAKE YOUR OWN
GPS Treasure Hunt

SUPPLIES

✴ GPS device, such as on a smartphone or a navigation device for a car

✴ several small objects to hide

✴ one or more friends

1 Ask your parents for permission to use a GPS device. First, practice using the GPS device on a trip to the grocery store. Type in the name or address of the store and put the device in the map view. As the car travels, follow where you are on the route. With your parents' help, figure out how to place a "tag" or "pin" on the device for a particular location. This will vary with the type of device. For example, on Google Maps on an iPhone, you touch and hold the location to add a pin. Tap the blue arrow on the pin, then tap "Add to Bookmarks." You can then pin more locations.

2 With your parents' permission, go to a large park or playground with a friend and the GPS device. Have your friend hide his or her eyes while you hide each of the small objects. When you hide each object, place a "tag" or "pin" on the GPS map for the location.

3 Ask your friend to find the objects using the GPS. Then reverse roles. Ask your friend to hide the objects and you find them. How close together can you hide objects and be able to distinguish them from each other on the GPS? Did this vary with whether the object was hidden under a tree or next to a wall?

What's Happening?

You can only get an accurate signal from a GPS satellite if there are no solid objects, such as walls or trees, between the GPS receiver and the satellite. Clouds don't affect the signal. The more satellites from which your receiver can get a signal, the more accurate the location reading will be.

ACTIVITY

MAKE YOUR OWN

Virtual Tour of the World

SUPPLIES

* computer with Internet browser
* Internet access

1 Ask your parents if it's okay to download and install Google Earth onto the computer. It is free and is located here: www.google.com/earth/download/ge/.

2 Click "Fly To" under the search button in the upper left corner. Enter your address in the search box. Double click the search results and you will "fly" home. You can view your house from above, or grab the orange figure on the right and drag it in front of your house to see a view from the street.

3 To find the exact latitude and longitude coordinates of your house or any other location, "fly to" the location, then click the placemark button (it looks like a push pin) in the toolbar at the top of the screen. Another screen will pop up, showing the latitude and longitude. You can also add a name and your own notes about the location if you like, then click "OK" to save the location as a place mark. If you want to see the imaginary latitude and longitude lines laid over the map, select "View" then "Grid."

UP, UP, AND AWAY!

DID YOU KNOW?

There are nearly one billion users of GPS worldwide—and growing!

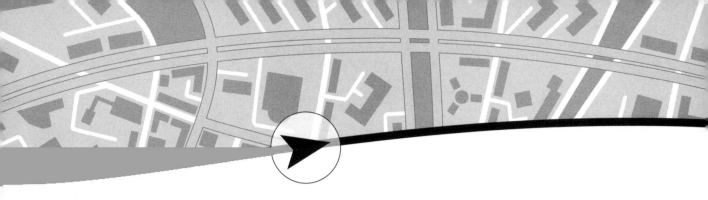

4 Visit some interesting places on earth. First, make sure "3D Buildings" is checked in the Layers panel in the lower left. Try typing in these addresses in the Fly To box, then zoom in or out or view at street level. Add a placemark for each place you like, so you can come back and visit later.

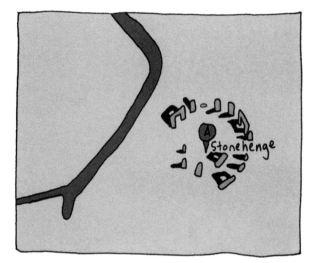

* ✱ Stonehenge, England

* ✱ Grand Canyon, Arizona

* ✱ Statue of Liberty, New York

* ✱ Great Pyramids, Cairo, Egypt

* ✱ Think of some other great places to visit!

What's Happening?

Google Earth has taken the data from Landsat images collected since 1972 and is making them available to the public in a way that is easy to use. All of the images are tied to exact latitude and longitudes so you can find the right place. Google Earth is continually developing new ways to look at the images, along with tours of places and scientific studies.

TRY THIS! Some people are worried that the increased use of GPS receivers in everyday items like cell phones will take away our privacy by making it too easy for people to know where we're going and what we're doing. What do you think? Can you think of ways that people can use GPS and have privacy too?

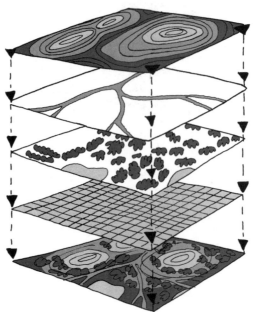

CHAPTER 5

What Is GIS?

A topographic map shows things on "top" of the land, like rivers, mountains, and other cultural and natural features of a region. It also shows the elevation of land, either using contour lines or shades of color to mark different elevations. But look out your window. There's a lot of stuff out there! You're probably looking at a street and other houses or apartments. You might see trees and telephone poles. If a topographic map is supposed to show everything on "top" of the land, how can there ever be enough room? The world is a big place. Can everything fit on a map? And what if one day you want to see all of the electrical lines on your street, but the next day you want to see changes in elevation?

WOrds2Know

GIS: stands for Geographic Information System. A system for storing and manipulating geographical information on a computer.

This is where Geographic Information System (**GIS**) comes in. GIS is a tool to help layer different types of information on a map. It links geographical data about where things are with other sources of information about what things are. GIS can reveal patterns and relationships we can't see on a normal road map or topographic map. You can look at a regular map to find where a road leads or where a lake would be. But a digital GIS map can tell you how long the road is and how many square miles the lake takes up.

Think of a GIS map as being like layers of a sandwich.

It uses longitude, latitude, and elevation from GPS as the key to link layers of information. A base map might come from satellite pictures or a topographic map. Then other information is placed on that base map in digital layers. There could be a layer showing information about buildings and addresses. Another layer might contain information about roads, electrical lines, or even underground water pipes.

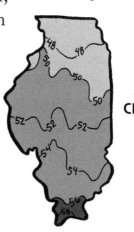

MAJOR ROADS

POPULATION

You can view all of the layers together, or just some of them, and you can keep adding or revising layers as new information comes in. Including the date and time is important on these maps. It helps us understand if we are viewing information from the same or different days and to look at changes over time.

APRIL CLIMATE

WOrds2Know

three dimensional: with depth, not just width and height.

What makes GIS so useful is that it enables the user to see and analyze all of that information **three dimensionally**. Sometimes just one glance at a map with extra information can tell you more than hours of looking through tables of data can.

John Snow and the First Use of GIS

In 1854, London was suffering from an outbreak of cholera, a deadly disease caused by bacteria in dirty water, milk, or food. No one could figure out where the disease came from or why it was spreading. An English doctor named John Snow began charting the spread of the disease on a map. He placed a dot on every home where a person had been infected. After his investigation, he noticed areas where the dots were clustered together. His map showed him that all of the dots were near a water pump. It turned out that this water pump was contaminated and causing the cholera to spread. The water pump was disconnected. This is considered the first use of mapping to help prevent disease. Snow's work would influence how future generations used GIS to help prevent disease and other natural dangers.

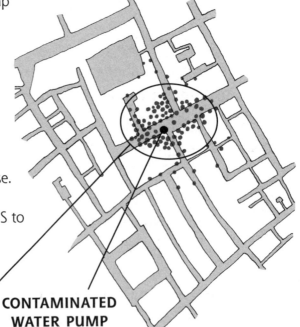

CLUSTER PATTERN OF OUTBREAKS

CONTAMINATED WATER PUMP

Who Uses GIS?

GIS is used by individuals, businesses, the military, and the government to help with many things, from urban planning to responding to emergencies. Here are some of the main ways people use GIS.

Population and the Census: The United States **Census** Bureau maintains information about the population of the country. This population data became the foundation of the GIS industry in the 1990s. A census is an official count of the population. In the United States, a census occurs every 10 years. Ask your parents if they've ever completed a census form. Sometimes these forms come in the mail. Other times a Census Bureau employee knocks on your door and asks questions about how many people live in the house and the age and level of education of each family member.

Knowing the number of people who live in a city or state is a good thing, but it's even better if that information can be **spatially** arranged.

> **WOrds2Know**
>
> **census:** an official count or survey of a population that records various details about individuals.
>
> **spatial:** viewed in a three-dimensional environment.

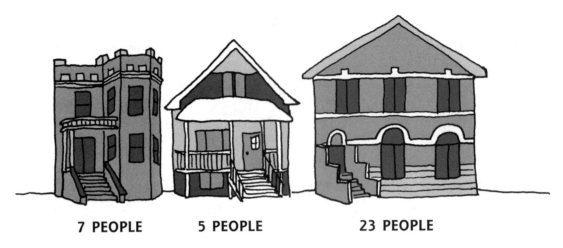

7 PEOPLE　　**5 PEOPLE**　　**23 PEOPLE**

The Census Bureau puts all of this information on a map to show how many people live in each city and neighborhood. The Census GIS can even show how many people live on your street or in your house! Police and emergency responders often connect their 9-1-1 to the Census-related GIS so they can quickly navigate to the source of a call and in and around neighborhoods.

City planners and businesses use maps of **population density** to make crucial decisions. How many schools should be in a town with a population density of 4,000 people per square mile? How many hospitals are needed? Once city planners know the specific size of a town and the number of people in it, they can make decisions about where to place schools, fire stations, and other buildings to best organize towns. Census maps also help transportation officials determine which neighborhoods need bus lines. Businesses use census data to make decisions about where to locate their stores, or how best to reach their customers.

Words2Know

population density: a measurement of the number of people in a given area, usually per square mile.

74

Shipping and Transportation: Did you know that the U.S. Postal Service delivers 212 billion pieces of mail a year? And they need to have all those addresses correct! The Postal Service has its own extensive GIS that details mail routes and addresses. They even use it to help track crime. If postal workers think the mail system is being used for something illegal, they'll track the activity and pinpoint addresses that might be involved. The police use similar GIS maps to identify criminal patterns.

Businesses of all kinds, especially shipping companies, use GIS to schedule the most **efficient** routes to ship packages. They also use GPS and GIS to track packages that are on the way. GIS can help shippers change their routes when there is construction on roads and plan when to increase the number of trucks in their fleet.

W🔘rds2Know

efficient: wasting as little time as possible in completing a task.

income: the amount of money someone makes.

▱ Where Would You Open a Toy Store? ↰

Imagine you want to open a toy store. Where will you put your store? GIS could help you look at detailed information to pick the best spot for your new business.

* **Population:** Can you find an area with a lot of families? How old are the kids in these families? How much **income** do these families have to spend on toys?

* **Competition:** Where are other toy stores located?

* **Transportation:** Is it going to be easy for customers to find and get to your store?

Emergency Response: GIS maps can help in emergencies such as fires, hurricanes, and floods. During wildfires, fire managers can see where fires are in real time and also view the terrain, vegetation, and centers of population. This helps them choose the best locations to put firefighters on the ground, or where to make **firebreaks**.

WOrds2Know

firebreak: a strip of cleared or plowed land used to stop the spread of a fire.

evacuation: immediate and rapid movement of people away from danger.

In January 2011, a massive flood hit the Queensland region of Australia. GIS was critical to the rescue effort. Rescue workers used GIS flood maps to see a real-time picture of rising water levels layered with the peaks and valleys of the land to pinpoint high-water areas. By also containing information on which roads were closed and the location of **evacuation** centers, these maps helped get people to safety as quickly as possible.

Environment: GIS has been a crucial tool to understanding the environment. It is especially useful to see how the environment has changed over time, and how some changes affect others.

Changes in forests have a wide impact. When too much forested land is cut for fuel, lumber, or farming, all aspects of the environment are affected.

Tree roots hold the soil together, so if there are fewer trees it weakens the soil. This can cause **erosion** and raise the risk of **landslides**.

Sometimes, GIS may show an increase in forestation. This is what's been happening in the eastern United States over the past two centuries. Areas that were once farmland have gone back to woodlands as people turned to occupations other than farming. This has benefits, but can also cause problems.

W*O*rds2Know

erosion: the gradual wearing away of rock or soil by water and wind.

landslide: when a mass of earth or rock slides down from a mountain or cliff.

digitize: to put data or information into digital form so that it can be processed by a computer.

Importance of Maps

In 2002, nine miners were working in the Quecreek Mine in Somerset County, Pennsylvania. They were 240 feet underground (73 meters) when they broke through the wall of an adjacent, abandoned mine. The abandoned mine had been flooded, and 72 million gallons of cold water rushed into Quecreek Mine (273 million liters). After 77 hours in frigid water and complete darkness, all nine miners were rescued in what is known as the Miracle of Quecreek. As city and mine officials wondered about how to prevent future disasters, one question kept coming up: could maps have prevented this near deadly accident?

The miners had been relying on an old, incomplete map. They had no idea there was an abandoned mine right next to them. The state of Pennsylvania now requires all mine owners to lend maps to the state for copying. The maps are scanned and **digitized** at the Institute for Mine Mapping at Indiana University of Pennsylvania and are available to the public. Over 30,000 mining maps have been collected and digitized. The hope is that by sharing better maps of all the mines in Pennsylvania, future disasters can be avoided.

More forest means more wildlife, but more wildlife means more damage to property near the forest. It's important to know both how much wildlife has increased, and where it is. It's much better, for example, to have deer on a huge tract of forested land than it is for them to be concentrated where there are also lots of people.

A GIS system can track all of these different elements to show changes in the environment over time. It can track changes in the soil, water, air, and **biological** activity, and represent these changes on a map. How else can GIS help environmental research? The possibilities are endless!

WOrds2Know

biological: having to do with something that is or was living, including plants, people, and animals.

reservoir: a natural or manmade body of water stored for future use.

species: a group of plants or animals that are related and look like each other.

- Monitoring sources of water such as **reservoirs** and ground water, and how they change over time.

- Creating real-time maps of oil spills and populations of endangered **species**.

- Tracking water samples taken in polluted rivers and how the pollutants have changed over time.

- Predicting changes to wildlife populations using information on forestation, human population, wildfires, plant species, and predators in the region.

- Tracking animals for research using GPS, then putting that information into a GIS to see how it relates to other information.

- Protecting endangered species by looking at changes in vegetation, rainfall, and other wildlife populations.

- Predicting the impact of a new road on a habitat.

ACTIVITY

MAKE YOUR OWN

Gis Map of a Park

SUPPLIES

* outside area with trees
* pad of graph paper
* pencil
* cloth measuring tape
* colored pencils in at least three colors

1 Select a location to map that has several trees, such as your backyard or a park. If possible, at least one of the trees should be an **evergreen** and at least one should be **deciduous**.

2 Draw the boundaries of the area on the paper. Put a small dot wherever there's a tree. Don't worry about being too exact about the locations.

3 For each tree, draw a circle around the dot and color it in. Use one color if the tree is evergreen, and another color if it is deciduous. Make the circle smaller if the tree is small, or larger if the tree is large.

4 Measure the circumference of each tree in inches or centimeters. Be sure to take all the measurements at the same height above the ground. Write the circumference next to the circle for each tree.

5 Using a different color of pencil, shade in every area that has grass. In areas where there is only a little grass, shade lightly, and where there is more grass, shade more heavily.

WOrds 2 Know

evergreen: a plant that keeps its leaves or needles throughout the year.

deciduous: a plant that sheds its leaves each year.

What's Happening?

Do you see a difference in the amount of grass around evergreen trees compared to deciduous trees, and around trees of larger circumference compared to trees of smaller circumference? Evergreens have droppings that make it harder for grass to grow underneath, while larger trees often have large roots that make it harder for grass to grow.

ACTIVITY

MAKE YOUR OWN
Gis Map for Aliens

SUPPLIES

* pad of paper
* pencil
* colored pencils
* ruler
* tracing paper
* tape

1 Make a simple map of your immediate neighborhood. Draw your street, your house, and at least one other house of someone you know. Lightly shade in areas with grass, and draw circles for trees.

2 Attach one piece of tracing paper to your base layer with tape along one edge. Lay the tracing paper flat so you can see the base layer beneath. Go outside and sit for a few minutes watching for birds. Count the number of birds and draw a symbol on the tracing paper for each bird. Put the symbols where you see the birds.

3 Using a different symbol for people, draw a symbol on the tracing paper for each person who lives at your house. Put the symbols where your family members are at the moment—don't forget to draw yourself sitting outside! If someone in your family isn't nearby, place the symbol where they might be on a typical day. Also draw each pet in your house, using a different symbol for pets. Do the same thing for the other houses. Make a guess where the people might be.

4 Tape a second piece of tracing paper on top of the first piece. Now imagine that it's midnight. Draw a symbol for each person and pet in your house where they would be at midnight. Draw a symbol for where you think each bird would be. Do the same for the other houses you've drawn.

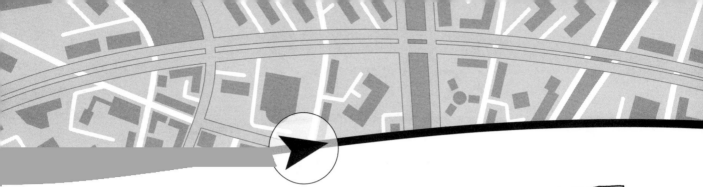

5 Imagine you're an alien who has come to earth to study its life forms. You don't know anything about humans, birds, or any other animals. You don't know how they interact or what they do during the day or night. Looking at the base map and tracing paper, what might you guess about the relationship between humans and birds? What about between humans and pets? What about their activities during the day or night?

What's Happening?

Looking at your layered map, an alien would see that humans and pets are close to each other at night and during the day. What would they think about the relationship between humans and pets compared to the relationship between humans and birds? If you were an alien, what other kind of information might you find useful to understand the relationship between humans and pets? Would it help to show that information on a map?

Scientists use information from GIS all the time to help determine relationships between different things. They might look at how ocean temperatures affect the types of animals that live there. Then they can see what happens when temperatures change. Or scientists can see how weather patterns affect the kinds of plants that can grow in an area, and how changing weather over time impacts plants.

ACTIVITY

SUPPLIES

❋ computer with Internet browser
❋ Internet access

USE THE LAYERS ON
*G*OOGLE *E*ARTH

1 If you don't already have Google Earth, ask your parents if it's okay to download and install it onto the computer. Google Earth is free and is located here: www.google.com/earth/download/ge/.

2 Click "Fly To" under the search button in the upper left corner. Enter "Japan" into the search box. Double click the search results and you'll be "flying" to Asia. In the lower left is the panel called Layers. Open different layers as noted to show additional information to answer the questions. Make sure the "3D Buildings" box is checked in the lower left of the Layers panel. Then follow these steps:

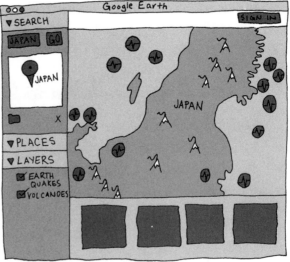

❋ Click the arrow next to "Gallery"

❋ Check the box "Earthquakes"

❋ Zoom in until you start to see the earthquake symbols. Can you see what look like long ditches in the Pacific Ocean? These trenches are where two tectonic plates are pushing together, causing earthquakes.

❋ Now check the "Volcanoes" box. Do they tend to occur in the same general area as earthquakes? Do you think they might be related?

❋ Leave the same boxes checked in the Layers panel, and this time "Fly To" Mount St. Helens. Zoom out a bit. Do you see lots of earthquakes and volcanoes? This is the other side of the Pacific Ocean, but there are tectonic plates coming together here, too.

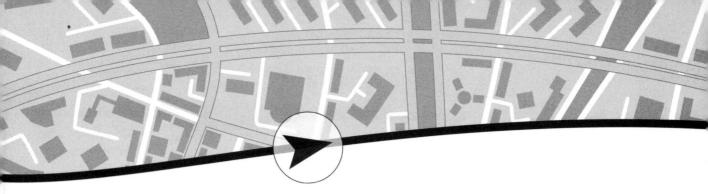

3 At the top of the Layers panel is a box with an arrow called Earth Gallery. It will take you to all sorts of maps and photos, from maps of earthquakes and how the earth looks at night to maps of postal codes or the Lewis and Clark expedition. If you click on "View" for a map and it doesn't take you to the map, you can open the map in your Internet browser by clicking on the button at the top that says "Open in [your Internet browser]."

What's Happening?

You have been using layers in Google Earth just like geographers do in other GIS systems. Seeing those layers together—like how volcanoes tend to be located near earthquakes and that both are often found near trenches—can help scientists develop theories about how the world works. When scientists were first developing the theory of plate tectonics, seeing the earthquakes in a ring around the Pacific Ocean helped them develop the theory. And they didn't have the complex GIS systems that we have today!

Take a look at the interior of Asia nowhere near an ocean. Do you see many symbols for earthquakes or volcanoes there? Why or why not?

DID YOU KNOW?

People have used Google Earth to make amazing discoveries, especially in remote areas of the earth. In 2010, Vincenzo de Michele discovered a 148-foot-wide crater from a meteorite in Egypt using Google Earth (45 meters wide). The crater is in a remote area of the Sahara Desert, which is why it hadn't been discovered before. Because it is especially well preserved, the crater will help scientists understand the hazards from meteorite impacts on the earth.

ACTIVITY

CHANGES OVER TIME ON

Google Earth

SUPPLIES

✳ computer with Internet browser

✳ Internet access

1 Look back at the last activity. Use the Layers feature on Google Earth to learn how to go to a location in Google Earth.

2 To view images from the past, click the Historical Imagery button in the toolbar at the top. To find the button, move your cursor over the buttons and the description will appear. The button looks like a clock. Move the slider at the top left corner to go back in time. Has your street changed much? What about other neighborhoods?

3 Fly to Las Vegas, Nevada. Zoom out a little until you can see Lake Mead to the right (east), which looks greenish-black. Move the historical slider to earlier times. How has Las Vegas changed over time? How has Lake Mead changed? Go to www.nomadpress.net/resources for a link to see a video of the changes over the 10 years from 1999 to 2010.

What's Happening?

Google Earth, Carnegie Mellon University, and the U.S. Geological Survey have been working to transfer Landsat images into videos and into the Historical Imagery buttons. You'll see from the Landsat images that Las Vegas has been a fast-growing city. At the same time, Lake Mead is shrinking. You might think that one caused the other, but that's not the case. Can you think of another reason Lake Mead could be shrinking?

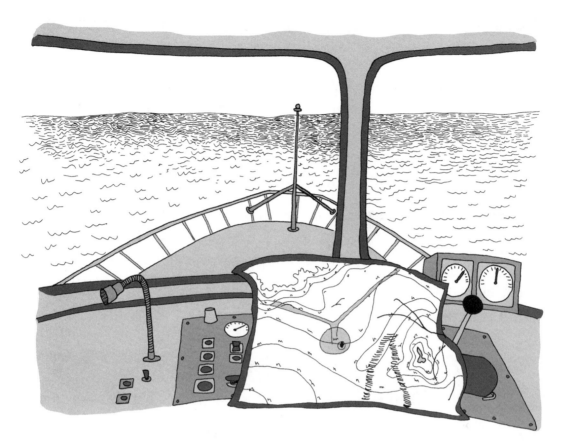

↗ CHAPTER 6 ↖

Oceans: The Least Known Surface on Earth

Did you know that 70 percent of the earth is covered
by water? The Pacific Ocean alone covers 30 percent!
But even though the oceans cover more than half of our
planet, we know surprisingly little about them. Half of
the earth's species live in the water, and some scientists
think there could be millions more that we don't even
know about. We know more about the topography
of the moon than we do about the ocean floor.

85

Having good maps is important for more than just navigation. Maps can also help us understand **tsunamis**, climate, and the overall health of the oceans. To understand the oceans, we need to know what's happening there—on top of the water and way down deep.

WOrds2Know

tsunami: a very large ocean wave, usually caused by an earthquake.

A nautical chart shows the surface of the ocean and safe travel routes. Since these charts can be updated with high-resolution satellite data, they are usually very accurate in the modern age.

Phantom Island

Nautical charts still aren't perfect. Until late 2012, a tiny island called Sandy Island was shown east of Australia in the Pacific Ocean. Sandy Island was on nearly every published map, including Google Earth and other electronic maps. When scientists studying the geology of the area went to find the island, there was nothing but deep water. This may not have been a mistake though! In the past, cartographers sometimes put small mistakes into their maps so they would know if someone stole their data. Mappers think Sandy Island was one such "mistake."

The Ocean Floor

Do you know where the tallest mountains are? What about the deepest valleys and largest plains? It's hard to believe, but all of these things are found at the bottom of the ocean floor.

Pretend for a minute that the oceans have been drained of all their water. What does the floor look like?

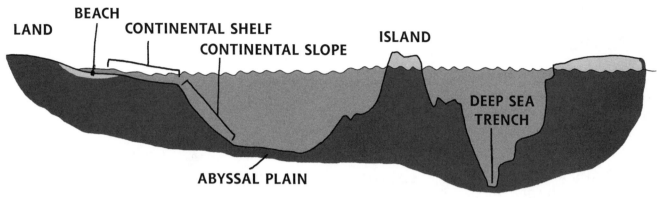

LAND
BEACH
CONTINENTAL SHELF
CONTINENTAL SLOPE
ISLAND
DEEP SEA TRENCH
ABYSSAL PLAIN

The **continental shelf** is located along the coast. The shelf is really a continuation of the continent off the coast. It continues until the ocean floor drops steeply at the **continental slope**. The continental slope goes down to the deep ocean basin, which is about 2½ to 3½ miles deep in most places (4 to 5½ kilometers). The ocean floor is also called the **abyssal plain**. It is a mostly flat layer of mud and **sediment** that stretches across the bottom of the ocean. Abyssal plains cover about 50 percent of the earth's surface. In places, there are huge drop-offs called **deep sea trenches**.

These trenches are the deepest parts of the ocean.

W**O**rds2Know

continental shelf: the extended perimeter of each continent below sea level until the land drops off steeply.

continental slope: the sharp decline from continental shelf to the deep ocean basin and abyssal plain.

abyssal plain: the underwater plain in the deep ocean basin.

sediment: dirt, fertilizer, rocks, and other tiny bits of matter deposited in rivers and oceans.

deep sea trench: the deepest parts of the ocean floor.

DID YOU KNOW? The National Oceanic and Atmospheric Agency (NOAA) has over 1,000 nautical charts covering 95,000 miles of coastline in the U.S. (153,000 kilometers). It's been making these charts since 1807.

Words 2 Know

mid-ocean ridge: an underwater mountain system.

submarine: under the surface of the sea. Also a ship that can dive deep underwater.

The ocean floor also has big mountains. Most underwater mountains are in long chains where two tectonic plates are spreading apart, called **mid-ocean ridges**. Others are individual mountains, usually formed from a **submarine** volcano. Volcanic eruptions happen every day in the deep ocean basin.

Submarine volcanic systems produce enough lava every year to fill an area nearly 10 times the size of Texas with 3 feet of lava (1 meter)!

The Deepest Place on Earth

The Mariana Trench goes down 7 miles below the surface of the ocean (11 kilometers). That makes it the deepest place on our planet. It's so deep that the peak of Mount Everest would be more than a mile underwater if it were dropped in. The pressure at the bottom is over 1,000 times the atmospheric pressure at sea level. The trench is located off the coast of the Mariana Islands in the western Pacific Ocean near Guam. It's shaped like a crescent, about 1,580 miles long (2,550 kilometers), but only about 43 miles wide (69 kilometers). Only two people have ever descended to the bottom of the trench, and that was in a single expedition in 1960.

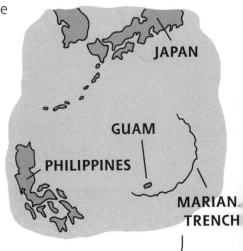

JAPAN

GUAM

PHILIPPINES

MARIANA TRENCH

DID YOU KNOW?

The global mid-ocean ridge is a submarine mountain chain that winds almost around the entire earth. It averages about 15,000 feet (4,500 meters) above the sea floor, higher than every mountain in the United States except Denali in Alaska. The mountain chain is more than 31,000 miles long (50,000 kilometers), which makes it the longest mountain chain on earth!

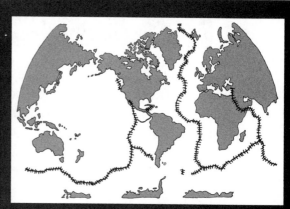

Bathymetric Charts

A **bathymetric chart** is like a topographical map for the ocean. It shows the water depth and the ocean floor. You can remember it by thinking of a bathymetric map like a "bath map."

WOrds2Know

bathymetric chart: a topographic map of terrain under the water.

Bathymetric charts have always been difficult to make, and still are today. That's because almost all of the ocean floor is miles deep. There's no light and the pressure is extremely high. Standard techniques of mapping from a distance, like using aerial photography or GPS or other radar, can't be used through water of that depth.

It has taken modern technology to map the ocean floor.

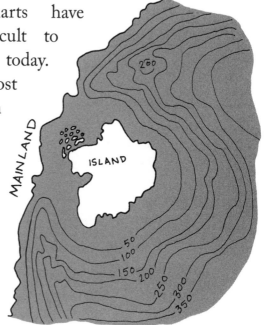

Hawaiian Mountains

Hawaii has three of the five tallest mountains. How? They start from about 18,000 feet below the ocean's surface (about 5,500 meters). Mauna Kea is the world's tallest mountain, though not the highest in elevation. It is also a volcano. It rises 13,796 feet above the surface of the ocean (4,205 meters) and about 32,000 feet from the bottom of the sea (9,750 meters). Mt. Everest in the Himalaya Mountains is the highest point on the earth at 29,035 feet above sea level (8,850 meters), but it is only the third-tallest mountain measured from base to summit.

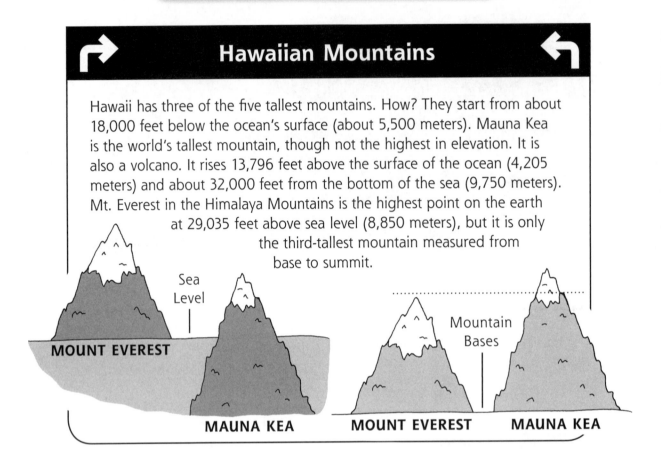

Sea Level

MOUNT EVEREST

MAUNA KEA

Mountain Bases

MOUNT EVEREST

MAUNA KEA

During the Age of Exploration, sailors used sounding lines to measure water depth. They dropped a weighted rope with knots into the water and counted how many knots went under the surface. But that only worked near the shore. Imagine measuring the ocean depths using rope!

Navigators slowly developed new techniques for deep-sea exploration. The military used early **sonar** during World War I to detect submarines. From there, sonar steadily improved for mapping deep waters.

WOrds2Know

sonar: a method of using sound pulses to detect objects and to measure the depth of water.

Sonar stands for <u>so</u>und <u>na</u>vigation and <u>r</u>anging. A sonar device sends sound signals through the water and tracks how long it takes for them to travel back. NOAA scientists use sonar to measure the depth of water and develop nautical charts. They can also locate underwater hazards, search for and map objects such as shipwrecks on the sea floor, and map the sea floor itself. Sonar is commonly used on submarines and fishing ships.

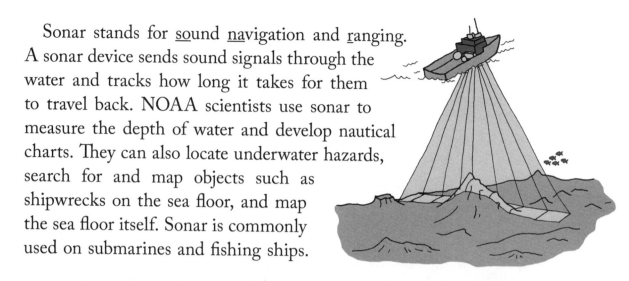

Ocean Depths

Ocean	Area	Average Depth	Deepest Point
Pacific	64,186,000 square miles/166,240,977 square kilometers	15,315 feet/4,668 meters	Mariana Trench (36,200 feet/11,034 meters below sea level)
Atlantic	33,420,000 square miles/86,557,403 square kilometers	12,881 feet/3,926 meters	Puerto Rico Trench (28,231 feet/8,605 meters below sea level)
Indian	28,350,000 square miles/73,426,163 square kilometers	13,002 feet/3,963 meters	Java Trench (25,344 feet/7,725 meters below sea level)
Southern	7,848,300 square miles/20,327,004 square kilometers	13,100–16,400 feet/3,993–4,999 meters	South Sandwich Trench (23,736 feet/7,235 meters below sea level)
Arctic	5,106,000 square miles/13,224,479 square kilometers	3,953 feet/1,205 meters	Eurasia Basin (17,881 feet/5,450 meters below sea level)

Try going into your school gymnasium and shouting hello. You'll hear a slight echo. What you're actually hearing is that final sound wave making its way back to you. The sound waves go from your mouth to the far wall and back.

In an ocean, the far wall is the ocean floor. A sonar system calculates how fast a sound wave should move through water and keeps track of how long it takes for sound waves to hit the ocean floor and bounce back.

TRY THIS! Have you ever done a cannonball into a pool? When you hit the water, waves travel outward to the edge of the pool. Then, when the waves hit the edge, they bounce back toward the spot where you hit the water. Sound waves from sonar operate in a similar way, even though you can't see them.

Animals and Sonar

Certain animals have sonar built into their brains and ears. Dolphins and killer whales are able to send out signals to map their location the same way a submarine does. They can tell the size, shape, and speed of objects in front of them. Dolphin skills are so accurate that they can even figure out what's in front of them.

Dolphins use **echolocation** by making little clicking sounds that travel through the water and bounce back to them. They have two small ear openings behind their eyes that can pick up the sound of the returning click. They also have an inner ear in their lower jaw that can detect its signal strength. Research has shown that dolphins wait for each click to return before clicking again. Dolphins can determine the shape and size of nearby objects by judging how long it takes the click to return and its signal strength.

WOrds2Know

echolocation: the biological sonar used by several types of animals to help locate and identify objects.

Most of the ocean floor has been mapped by now, but not always in a way that is useful. Much of the mapping is done with satellites. Satellites can measure extremely small differences in **gravity**, which changes when there's a mountain beneath the surface of the ocean. Satellites give us a good idea of large features on the ocean floor, but only at a resolution of 6 miles (10 kilometers). This means that an object that is less than 6 miles across isn't distinguishable on a map. We can't pick it out in an image. But knowing where the biggest changes are helps to pinpoint where more detailed surveying needs to happen.

WOrds 2 Know

gravity: a force that pulls all objects toward the earth.

cargo: goods carried by ship, truck, train, or airplane.

Getting better resolution requires either being closer to the image or using better equipment. Some ships carry sonar devices and travel back and forth in a line, much like a lawn mower, mapping as they go. In some places ships tow tiny submarines that travel close to the ocean floor to make maps at a resolution of 3 feet (1 meter). On the continental shelf, maps can have a resolution down to 2 inches (5 centimeters). But mapping to this accuracy over all the oceans would take hundreds of years and tens of billions of dollars.

DID YOU KNOW? Over 90 percent of the world's **cargo** is carried by ships.

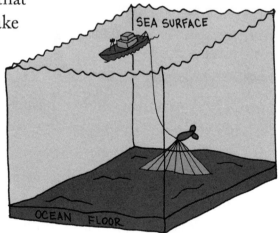

Marie Tharp

For many years, people thought that the ocean floor was just a flat floor of sediment and mud. Most scientists thought it was too cold, too dark, and too pressurized to support much life. Marie Tharp and Bruce Heezen analyzed a lot of data about the ocean floor and determined that there was an enormous series of mountains on the floor of the Atlantic Ocean. The maps Tharp made became the first to show the Mid-Atlantic Ridge, which is the longest mountain range in the world. In 1977, she published the first map to show the topographic features of the world's oceans. Tharp was a groundbreaking cartographer whose work still influences the field of oceanography and plate tectonics today.

Navigating the Deep Seas

WOrds2Know

scuba: a container of air connected to a mouthpiece, used for swimming underwater. Stands for self-contained underwater breathing apparatus.

oceanographer: a scientist who studies the ocean.

Outside of a ship, humans cannot go very deep, even using **scuba** gear. Besides the dark and the cold, the biggest problem is the pressure. The deepest we can go is about 1,000 feet (305 meters), and even then, there isn't much time for looking around.

One way humans have explored the deep seas is in Deep Submergence Vehicles (DSVs).

A DSV is a deep-diving manned submarine. It is self-propelled so that whoever is inside can direct the DSV where to go. They help **oceanographers** explore marine life and improve their maps and charts. They can also be used for rescue missions for sunken ships and submarines.

Remotely Operated Underwater Vehicles (ROVs), which don't carry a human on board, have mostly replaced DSVs. ROVs are connected by a thick cable to a ship on the surface and are operated by a person on the ship. ROVs are a little bit like remote-control cars, only these vehicles can go thousands of feet deep. Since they don't require a human to dive deep down into the ocean, ROVs are considered safer than DSVs.

ROVs usually have a camera on the front that helps with steering and navigating. But these cameras can also record video of the deepest regions of the sea. A powerful lighting system makes the footage visible and clear. ROVs also have equipment to take samples, measure temperature and light, and take depth measurements using sonar.

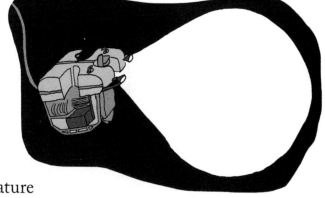

↱ Jacques Cousteau ↰

Jacques Cousteau was the most famous underwater explorer of the twentieth century. As a former member of the French Navy, he became fascinated with underwater exploration. He turned a British Royal Navy minesweeper into a research vessel called *Calypso*, and equipped it with underwater laboratories to help him study the ocean.

One of his first major breakthroughs was the Aqua-lung, which allowed divers to stay underwater for hours. This eventually led to the scuba gear and oxygen tanks we see today. Cousteau also developed a waterproof camera and produced three full-length movies about the oceans. His work educated the public on the oceans and what life is really like for underwater creatures. In 1985, Cousteau was awarded the Presidential Medal of Freedom, which is the highest honor the U.S. government awards to someone not in the military.

ROVs are used by the military to find old mines and ships. The oil and gas industry uses them to inspect pipelines and oil platforms, and scientists use them for research.

Before ROVs, scientists studied marine animals by catching them in nets. But nets only hold onto hard–bodied animals, like **crustaceans**. When **gelatinous** animals with jelly-like bodies are caught in nets, they disintegrate when brought to the surface. Scientists now think that about 40 percent of the **biomass** in the deep ocean is gelatinous.

Together, DSVs and ROVs have allowed researchers to observe some unusual animals in their habitats.

WOrds 2 Know

crustacean: an animal such as a crab or shrimp with a hard outer shell, jointed limbs, and two sets of antennae.

gelatinous: jelly-like.

biomass: the total mass of living matter within a given area.

thermal vent: a groove in the earth's surface that emits very hot water heated from deep within the earth.

- Osedax worms that eat the bones of dead whales.

- "Bumpy" jelly, with wart-like bumps of stinging cells on the jelly's feeding arms and bell.

- The Yeti crab, living in deep-sea **thermal vents**. This blind, deep-sea crab has legs covered by long, yellow hairs with dense colonies of bacteria living on its hairs. They have been observed holding their arms out over the plumes of warm water in the vents. Scientists speculate that they might be cultivating the bacteria as a food source.

Even with sonar and submersible ships, the ocean remains a tricky place to map. There will always be mysteries and new places to explore. Maybe one day you'll help lead the way in developing new deep-sea maps!

ACTIVITY

TRY YOUR OWN
*E*CHOLOCATION

SUPPLIES

* blindfold
* a friend
* frying pan
* thick fabric

1 Close your eyes and put on the blindfold. Have a friend stand in front of you and hold a frying pan in front of your face.

2 Make noises of some kind, like clicks with your tongue, whistling, or singing. As you make the noises, have your friend move the frying pan closer or farther away. Try to guess whether the pan is closer or farther. Keep practicing until you can guess.

3 Now have your friend hold the frying pan about a foot away from your face (30 centimeters). Make noises while your friend holds the fabric up in front of the pan, then takes it away. Try to guess when the pan is bare and when it is covered in fabric.

4 Have your friend lead you down a hall with open doors on both sides. Make noises as you walk and see if you can tell when you pass by an open door. Switch places and give your friend a chance to try echolocation.

What's Happening?

You probably aren't aware of it, but you are hearing the echo of the sound from the frying pan. How do you think this happens? Even though you can't quite pick out the echo, your brain still detects it and can get a rough idea of the distance of the pan.

ACTIVITY

MAKE YOUR OWN

*S*ONAR

SUPPLIES

* a wide bowl
* thin plastic wrap
* salt
* metal pan
* large metal spoon
* water
* eyedropper

1 Stretch the plastic wrap tightly over the bowl. Sprinkle a few shakes of salt onto the plastic wrap.

2 Bang the metal spoon onto the pan right over the salt. Does the salt jump or vibrate?

3 Take off the salt and plastic wrap and fill the bowl almost full with water. From about a foot above the water, use the eyedropper to squirt a drop of water into the center. Watch the surface of the water closely. Do you see waves moving outward from where the drop hit the water? What happens when the wave hits the side of the bowl?

What's Happening?

Sound is a series of waves of pressure that are carried through air, water, or a solid. We hear sound because of how the waves hit our ear drum and cause it to vibrate. When sound waves hit an object, the vibrations are usually too small to see. The plastic wrap acts like an eardrum or a sensor on a sonar device.

When you squirt the drop of water into the bowl of water, the wave it makes is similar to a sound wave. It travels out from the middle and then bounces back from the side. This is very similar to what happens when sound waves from a sonar device hit the bottom of the ocean. What would happen if there was a very large mountain there?

ACTIVITY

MAKE YOUR OWN
*B*ATHYMETRIC *M*AP

1 You and a friend each take a shoebox. Coat the bottom with clay as if it is the bottom of the ocean. Make at least one mountain between 1 and 3 inches high, as well as a flat area and a trench. Don't look at each other's box.

2 Use the ruler to draw a grid of 1-inch squares (2½ centimeters) on the lid. Poke a hole in the middle of each square. Place the lids on top of the boxes.

3 Switch boxes with your friend. Hold the wooden skewer straight up and down by the pointy end and poke it through one of the holes. Lower the rod until it just touches the clay, but don't push it into the clay. Mark the depth with your finger. Pull the rod out and measure it to the nearest quarter inch (half centimeter). Write the measurement directly on the shoebox lid in the square where you poked the wooden rod. Repeat this step for all of the squares on the lid.

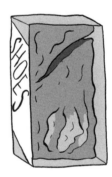

4 Look at your numbers. Try to predict where the mountain, trench, and flat areas are. The mountain will be where the numbers are smaller, because the rod didn't reach as far down. Draw contour lines by connecting numbers of similar values. Remember that contour lines never cross. Take the lid off. Is the topography similar to what you predicted?

What's Happening?

Your wooden rod is like a sounding line. It is also like a sound wave that is sent down to bounce off the ocean floor. What happens in real life if a current pushes on a sounding line and what might sailors do to help a rope sink straight down?

CHAPTER 7

Space: Navigating the Final Frontier

The celestial bodies in **outer space** have always been an important navigational tool. Ancient explorers relied on celestial navigation to travel the seas and make maps. The universe is vast and it takes powerful tools to map and explore the planets, the stars, and beyond.

But mapping the heavens in detail, and actually going there, is much harder to accomplish. It has required many new tools and new technologies, which are still improving. Nonetheless, we keep looking for answers to some of the same questions the ancient explorers asked.

What can other objects in the sky tell us about our own planet? How can we better map them? What's really out there? Astronomers rely on telescopes to peer into our **solar system** and spacecraft to explore farther out into the unknown.

W rds2Know

outer space: the physical universe beyond earth's atmosphere.

solar system: the collection of eight planets, moons, and other celestial bodies that orbit the sun.

Telescopes

Humans have always observed the sun, planets, and stars with their eyes. When telescopes were invented in 1608 by three people in three different places, observation took a great leap forward. It wasn't long before Galileo discovered that Jupiter has moons, the sun has spots, and the moon has hills and valleys. The heavens became real, and the heavenly bodies became places that could be mapped!

The first telescopes were refracting telescopes, which bend light so it comes together at a single point—your eye. Refracting telescopes, especially shorter ones, can have blurry images.

REFRACTING TELESCOPE

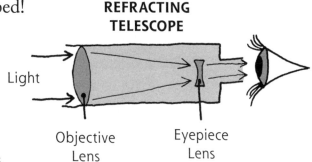

Light

Objective Lens

Eyepiece Lens

REFLECTING TELESCOPE

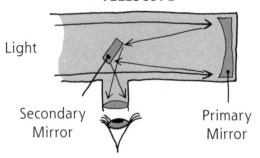

Light

Secondary Mirror

Primary Mirror

WOrds 2 Know

electromagnetic spectrum: the entire range of radiation that includes high-energy cosmic rays and gamma rays, x-rays, radio waves, short microwaves, ultraviolet and infrared light, and visible light.

In 1683, Isaac Newton built the first reflecting telescope, which uses curved mirrors to reflect light and form an image. At first reflecting telescopes weren't much clearer than refracting ones, but over time they have been refined to give extremely good images.

DID YOU KNOW?

Before the invention of the reflecting telescope, telescopes were often very long. In the late seventeenth century, some telescopes were as long as 600 feet (180 meters)!

No telescope can give a perfect image in all types of light and at all distances, so different designs work better for certain types of sky viewing. All major telescopes used today in astronomy are reflecting. Visible light is just one part of the **electromagnetic spectrum**. A fire, for example, gives off visible light, but it also emits invisible infrared, or heat. Objects in space emit electromagnetic waves in many parts of the spectrum, from radio and microwaves to cosmic and gamma waves. There are devices to collect information from all of these sources.

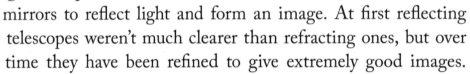

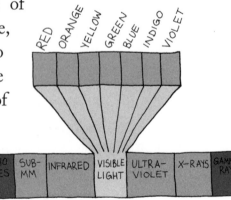

The Range of Radiation

Spaceships

- - - - - - - - - - - -

Astronomers have used many satellites, rockets, probes, and **rovers** to explore the solar system and outer space. Between the lack of air and gravity, space is a difficult place for humans, so nearly all these spacecraft are unmanned. Space is also a difficult place to navigate. A compass won't work in space! Spacecraft often rely on gyroscopes to keep track of their shifts in direction and distance traveled.

TRY THIS!  Look up at the stars. Do they look like they're twinkling? They're not. It's actually earth's atmosphere distorting the image, a bit like looking at something through a glass of water. Astronomers often cope with this distortion by placing their telescopes at high altitudes so there's less atmosphere to look through.

W**O**rds**2**Know

> **rover:** a slow-moving vehicle used to explore planets.
>
> **star tracker:** an instrument that logs star positions to aid in navigation.

Spacecraft also use **star trackers** to determine their position. A star tracker is a kind of space camera that is constantly recording the location of stars. It tells a spacecraft where it is in relation to stars.

Spacecraft can capture pictures from extreme distances, or get close to the outer planets for a detailed look. And because spacecraft can travel above the earth's atmosphere, the pictures and data they collect aren't distorted.

The combination of telescopes and spacecraft has provided some of the most exciting discoveries about our universe.

The Hubble Telescope

The Hubble Space Telescope was launched in 1990. The size of a large school bus, it is the first space-based **optical** telescope. It has provided

* Spectacular pictures of stars and **galaxies** of all shapes and colors.

* A better estimate of the age of our universe at about 13.8 billion years old.

* A look into very deep space.

* Pictures of the collision of a comet with Jupiter.

* Evidence of planets around other stars.

By observing the formation of stars and planets in other galaxies, the Hubble Space Telescope has given us a window into how solar systems, including our own, form.

WOrds2Know

optical: built to assist sight.

galaxy: a collection of star systems held together by gravity.

Our Solar System

At the center of our solar system is its largest star, the sun. The sun is approximately 90 million miles away from the earth (145 million kilometers) and is 109 times wider. It is 11,000 degrees Fahrenheit (6,093 degrees Celsius) on the surface of the sun!

There are eight planets that orbit our sun. The four inner planets are Mercury, Venus, Earth, and Mars. These are known as terrestrial planets, meaning that they are made mostly of metals and rocks. Terrestrial planets can have canyons, craters, mountains, and volcanoes. Because terrestrial planets are closer to Earth, they are easier to study than the outer planets.

In 1959, an 84-foot antenna (26 meters) beamed a radar signal to Venus and caught the echo five minutes later. Scientists could then calculate that Venus was 28 million miles away (45 million kilometers). And now, we're landing rovers directly on Mars.

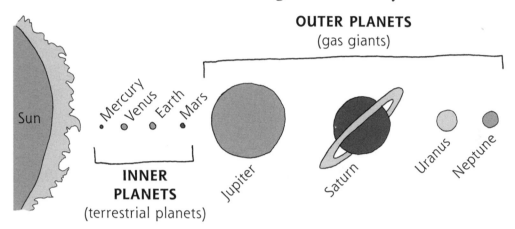

OUTER PLANETS
(gas giants)

Sun

Mercury · Venus · Earth · Mars

Jupiter

Saturn

Uranus

Neptune

INNER PLANETS
(terrestrial planets)

The outer planets of Jupiter, Saturn, Uranus, and Neptune are trickier to study. These huge gas giants have thick atmospheres of hydrogen and helium gases. Most scientists think the outer planets don't have solid surfaces. Though they are extremely far from Earth, we can sometimes see Jupiter and Saturn appear as bright colors in the night sky, even without a telescope.

For decades, starting in 1930, Pluto was considered the ninth planet. In 2006, however, most astronomers decided that Pluto, which is only about one-third the

DID YOU KNOW?

Saturn and Jupiter together have at least 128 moons. Titan, Saturn's largest moon, has a thick atmosphere and is larger than the planet Mercury!

size of our own moon, was too small to be considered a planet. They reclassified it as a dwarf planet. Pluto is located beyond Neptune in a belt of other objects called the Kuiper Belt.

Exploring Mars

Mars is often called the Red Planet because it is covered in dark red dust. It's a fascinating place with a volcanic mountain over 16 miles high (25 kilometers), the tallest mountain on any planet in the solar system! Mars has ice on it today, and there is evidence that there was liquid water in the past. Just about anywhere we find water on Earth, there is also life. Could there have been microscopic life on Mars in the past? Could there be today?

NASA wanted to know. On August 5, 2012, NASA's *Curiosity* rover landed on Mars. *Curiosity* is a car-sized robot designed to withstand the harsh climate of Mars. It is guided by commands sent from Earth every day, moving very slowly to protect it from damage as it travels over rough terrain.

WOrds2Know

NASA: National Aeronautics and Space Administration. The U.S. organization in charge of space exploration.

Curiosity's main goal is to determine if Mars could have ever supported life.

The rover collects and analyzes samples of rock and soil to detect the mineral carbon, which is the main building block for life. It will also gather information about climate and geology. The mission's findings will help future exploration on Mars, perhaps even preparing for a human to travel there.

The rover *Opportunity*, which arrived on Mars in January 2004, is still exploring the red planet. NASA engineers expected it to last about 90 martian days (one earth day plus 39½ minutes). But, it's still going more than nine years later! That's impressive given the rough terrain and daily temperature changes of 100 degrees.

Exploring Jupiter and Saturn

The *Juno* spacecraft is on its way to Jupiter. Launched in August 2011, *Juno* is scheduled to arrive in July 2016 and will orbit the planet for one year. It will be the first time anyone has seen beneath Jupiter's dense cover of clouds. Scientists are hoping to learn more about how Jupiter formed.

Earth Flyby
October 2013

Launch
August 2011

EARTH

Deep Space Maneuvers
August/September 2012

Jupiter Orbit
August 2016

WOrds2Know

geyser: a natural spring that shoots water into the air.

In October 1997, the *Cassini* launched toward Saturn. In 2004, it entered Saturn's orbit and began exploring the beautiful planet and its atmosphere, rings, and moons. It found that ice **geysers** erupting from its moon Enceladus created one of Saturn's rings. *Cassini* will continue its current mission until September 2017.

DID YOU KNOW?

There's oxygen on Saturn's moon Dione, but the atmosphere is about 5 trillion times less dense than it is on Earth. That, plus the fact that the average temperature there is -121 degrees Fahrenheit (-186 degrees Celsius) means that it may not be the best place to go for vacation.

Mapping the Mysteries of Space and Time

How do you measure space? Not just in our solar system, but way beyond it to other galaxies where spaceships will probably never go. You can't use a measuring tape. Next time you're out riding in a car at night on a dark road, try guessing how far away an oncoming car is by looking at its headlights. You might guess that a car is farther away if the lights are dim or small. That's similar to what astronomers do: they use the brightness of stars and objects to estimate their distance from us.

A certain kind of star, called a Cepheid variable star, expands and contracts in a regular pattern. As it does, its brightness also changes. But all of these stars reach a similar maximum brightness. So astronomers can look at how bright a variable star appears from earth at any given time and use that to figure out how far away it is. This technique has been used to measure distances up to 60 million **light years** away!

Words 2 Know

light year: the distance that light travels in one year, equal to about 5.88 trillion miles (9.46 trillion kilometers).

IF 1 LIGHT YEAR = 6 TRILLION MILES... HOW FAR IS ONE MILLION LIGHT YEARS?

DID YOU KNOW?

A light year might sound like it's a measure of time, but it's also a measure of distance. One light year is the distance that light travels in one year. It's about 6 trillion miles (10 trillion kilometers).

To measure space is to also measure time. When you look through a telescope, you are looking back in time. That's because when we see the light from a star that's a million light years away, it means that it took the light a million years to travel to us. So we're looking at the star as it appeared a million years ago. What is that star like right now? We'll have to wait another million years for its light to reach us to find out! Astronomers use this fact to peer at places extremely far away, as they were extremely long ago.

DID YOU KNOW?

Astronomers estimate that there are more than 80 billion galaxies in the universe.

In December 2012, astronomers announced that the Hubble Space Telescope had discovered seven galaxies over 13 billion light years away from us.

The Strangeness of Space

Mapping the heavens has shown us some very strange things about our universe. Astronomers have to use clues to figure out what's really going on. If you see footprints in the snow, you know someone walked there after it snowed—without actually seeing the person walk. It's the same in space. But it's very hard to map. It's a little like being told you have to map someone's living room, but your eyes and ears are covered and you're not allowed to use your hands. Here are some strange things scientists have discovered:

Black Holes: One strange space object that no one can actually see is a black hole. A black hole is actually the opposite of a hole. It is a place in space so densely packed with matter that its gravity pulls everything into it with so much force even light can't escape.

Scientists can see that a star approaching a black hole breaks apart and is pulled in toward the black hole. Black holes often occur when a very large star is dying or has died and all the matter from that star squeezes into a tiny space. A star 10 times as massive as our own sun would fit into a sphere as wide as New York City.

Dark Matter: Dark matter is another type of matter that gives off no light. It can't be seen but is believed to make up as much as 85 percent of the mass of the universe. So how do we know it's out there? Because there's not enough gravitational pull among all the visible stars in a galaxy to hold it together. The stars should be flying off into space. But they're not.

So there's something else acting on those stars like invisible glue. That's the gravitational force from something that has mass but that we can't see. We call it dark matter. Astronomers have mapped it in space using clues—such as bright images of huge clusters of galaxies held inside dark regions—that show it's like a spider's web throughout the universe.

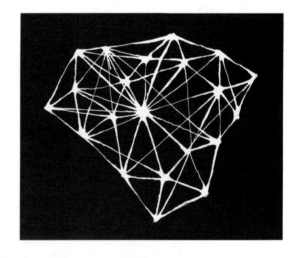

Dark Energy: Even stranger than dark matter is dark energy. Some energy, like light and heat from the sun, can be seen or measured directly. Just as with dark matter, we can't see dark energy. Scientists don't even agree that it exists, although most think it does, thanks to the Hubble Space Telescope.

Where's the Light?

When scientists think about mass and energy, they think of them as interchangeable. That's because mass can be converted into energy, or energy into mass. Think of a log burning. Some of it turns to ashes, but most of it is converted into energy that we observe as light and heat. When you think of the universe this way, about 70 percent of the mass-energy is dark energy and about 25 percent of the mass-energy is dark matter. That leaves only about 5 percent for everything that we can see and feel.

Perhaps the most astounding discovery made by the Hubble Space Telescope was related to the expansion of the universe. Astronomers have known for some time that the universe is expanding. They thought, however, that gravity was causing the rate of expansion to slow down over time. But measurements from the Hubble Telescope show that the opposite is happening.

In fact, the universe's expansion is speeding up! Scientists speculate that some force or energy is pulling the universe apart. That energy is called dark energy. And it makes up most of the energy in the universe.

 WOrds2Know

amateur: someone who does something for enjoyment and not as a job.

 **TRY THIS!**

You might think that mapping the heavens is for experts only. But star gazing is as easy as simply looking up. Many **amateurs** take it further by using telescopes and tracking stars and asteroids. Some have discovered comets or been the first to see explosions on planets. We still know very little about space and the planets. Maybe you'll be part of the next discoveries!

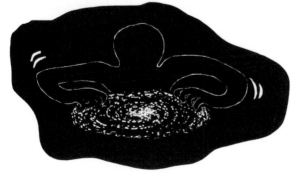

ACTIVITY

EXPAND YOUR

$\mathcal{U}$NIVERSE

SUPPLIES

* graph paper
* pencil
* large rubber band
* 7 paperclips
* partner
* ruler with centimeters

In October 2012, NASA's *Spitzer* Space Telescope measured the speed of the universe's expansion at a rate of a little more than 46.2 miles per second (74.3 kilometers per second) per megaparsec. A megaparsec is roughly 3 million light years. That's really fast! Explore what happens to the planets during expansion.

1 Using the graph paper, make a 5-column table with headings, Paperclip #, From Center to Paperclip #, Distance Before Expansion, Distance After Expansion, and Difference. Going down the left side of the table, indicate each paperclip number in order with the paperclip farthest left being #1.

2 Make a cut through the rubber band and clip the paperclips onto the rubber band spaced roughly equally apart. Paperclip #1 should be exactly in the center of the rubber band. Ask your partner to hold the elastic band without stretching it, but so it is straight. Measure the distance in centimeters from the center to each paperclip and record the measurements in the table.

3 Ask your partner to stretch the rubber band. Now measure again from the center paperclip to each of the others and record the distances in the table.

4 For each paperclip, calculate the difference between the Before Expansion and After Expansion measurements. Record them in the Difference column. Plot each point on a graph with the x-axis as the Beginning Distance and the y-axis the Difference.

What's Happening?

As the paperclips get farther apart, do they maintain the same distance relative to one another? This is how the universe expands.

ACTIVITY

MAKE YOUR OWN
Solar System

SUPPLIES

* markers
* index cards
* 2 rolls of toilet paper
* masking tape

1 Write the names of each planet listed below and the sun on individual index cards. On one card, write the following scale. This scale is based on the diameter of the sun being 0.2 inches across (½ centimeter). Each number represents how many toilet paper squares the planet is from the sun, rounded to the closest half-square.

* Mercury.............2
* Venus...............3.5
* Earth..............5
* Mars................7.5

* Jupiter.............25.5
* Saturn.............47
* Uranus...........94
* Neptune..........148

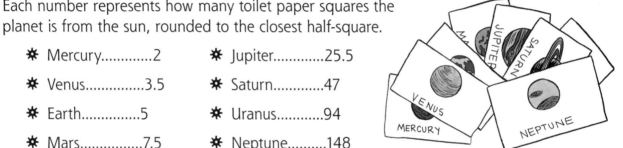

2 Go to a dry place where you can unroll most of a roll of toilet paper and lay it flat, such as a sidewalk outside. Place the card for the sun on the ground or floor.

3 Next to the sun, tape down an end of the toilet paper and begin unrolling. When you have unrolled two squares of paper, place the card for Mercury on the paper and keep unrolling. Place the cards for each of the planets at the correct number of squares.

4 Make a small dot on each card to show the size of each planet. With this scale, all but the sun would be a small dot. Even Jupiter is only 0.2 inches across!

What's Happening?

Most pictures of the solar system show the planets greatly enlarged compared to how far apart they are, so we can see their details. But in reality, the planets are VERY far apart. Alpha Centari is the closest visible star to our sun, about 25 trillion miles away (40 trillion kilometers). Using our toilet paper scale, that would be about 91 miles away (146 kilometers), or well over 1 million toilet paper squares.

ACTIVITY

MAKE YOUR OWN
GYROSCOPE

SUPPLIES

- ✳ 2 pairs of gloves
- ✳ front bicycle wheel with a quick-release hub
- ✳ a friend
- ✳ oven mitt
- ✳ chair that swivels

Satellites use gyroscopes to navigate. A gyroscope is a spinning wheel, or set of wheels, on a platform. The platform is free to rotate, but the wheel maintains position. When an aircraft or satellite moves, the wheel spins in the same position. Sensors detect the difference in the two positions to tell when a ship has changed direction. A spinning bicycle wheel can be a simple gyroscope.

1 Put on the gloves. Hold the wheel upright in front of you, with one hand on each side of the axle so the wheel can spin freely. Try tilting the wheel to the left, then bring it back to vertical and tilt the wheel to the right.

2 With the wheel vertical, have your friend spin the wheel fast. Tilt the wheel to the left and to the right as it spins. Is it hard? Have your friend put on the oven mitt and stop the spinning.

3 Sit on the swivel chair while holding the wheel vertical. Have your friend spin the wheel fast. Tilt the wheel to the left. Does the chair move? Now tilt the wheel to the right. What happens to the chair?

What's Happening?

The spinning wheel resists moving because of angular momentum. The more angular momentum, the more it wants to spin in the same direction. How does this explain what happens when your hands switch positions while you are sitting in the chair? Why does a spinning wheel resist changing the plane it is spinning in?

Gyroscopes also provide stability for vehicles. A moving bicycle stays upright because of angular momentum. In the same way, the Mars Rovers can tackle rough, unknown terrain because of the stabilizing influence of gyroscopes.

abyssal plain: the underwater plain in the deep ocean basin.

accelerometer: a device used to measures acceleration.

aerial: relating to the air.

aeronautical chart: a map designed to assist in the navigation of an airplane.

Age of Exploration: a period from the early 1400s to the early 1600s when Europeans explored and mapped the world.

altitude: the height of something above the level of the sea. Also called elevation.

amateur: someone who does something for enjoyment and not as a job.

annotated map: a map with descriptions or explanations.

antenna: a metal rod that sends and receives radio waves.

astrolabe: a Greek instrument used to determine the position of the sun and stars.

astronomer: a person who studies objects in the sky such as the sun, moon, planets, and stars.

atlas: a book of maps or charts.

atmospheric pressure: the amount of force pressing down on you by the weight of the air.

atom: the smallest particle of matter in the universe that makes up everything, like tiny building blocks or grains of sand.

atomic clock: an extremely accurate timekeeping device controlled by the vibrations of atoms.

axis of rotation: an imaginary line through a planet's poles, around which it rotates.

barometer: a scientific instrument used to measure air pressure.

bathymetric chart: a topographic map of terrain under the water.

BCE: put after a date, BCE stands for Before Common Era and counts down to zero. CE stands for Common Era and counts up from zero.

beacon: a fire or light set in a visible location as a warning or signal.

biological: having to do with something that is or was living, including plants, people, and animals.

biomass: the total mass of living matter within a given area.

broadcast: to send out signals to be received by radio or television receivers.

cargo: goods carried by ship, truck, train, or airplane.

cartographer: a person who makes maps.

celestial body: a star, planet, moon, or object in the sky.

census: an official count or survey of a population that records various details about individuals.

century: 100 years.

chart: to make a map or detailed plan.

circumference: the distance around something. The circumference of the earth is the distance around its widest point, called the equator.

climate: average weather patterns in an area over a long period of time.

Colonial America: the name given to America when talking about the years 1607–1776 when new settlers came from Europe and before the United States became its own country.

compass: a device that uses a magnet to show which direction is north.

conformal map: a map that preserves the angles between locations.

conserve: to use something carefully, so it doesn't get used up.

constellation: a group of stars that form a recognizable pattern or design.

Continental Divide: a ridge of mountains running from northwestern Canada through Mexico that separates the waters that flow into the Atlantic Ocean or Gulf of Mexico from those that flow into the Pacific Ocean.

continental shelf: the extended perimeter of each continent below sea level until the land drops off steeply.

continental slope: the sharp decline from continental shelf to the deep ocean basin and abyssal plain.

contour lines: lines on a map that show changes in elevation.

coordinates: numbers used to determine the position of a point, line, or surface.

crustacean: an animal such as a crab or shrimp with a hard outer shell, jointed limbs, and two sets of antennae.

culture: a group of people and their beliefs and way of life.

current: the steady flow of water in one direction.

dead reckoning: a method of determining a ship's position by using a previously determined position and the distance traveled.

deciduous: a plant that sheds its leaves each year.

deep sea trench: the deepest parts of the ocean floor.

destination: the place to which you are going.

digitize: to put data or information into digital form so that it can be processed by a computer.

distort: to make something look different from its normal shape.

echolocation: the biological sonar used by several types of animals to help locate and identify objects.

ecosystem: a community of plants and animals living in the same area and relying on each other to survive.

efficient: wasting as little time as possible in completing a task.

electromagnetic spectrum: the entire range of radiation that includes high-energy cosmic rays and gamma rays, x-rays, radio waves, short microwaves, ultraviolet and infrared light, and visible light.

elevation: the height above sea level.

environmental: relating to the natural world and the impact of human activity on its condition.

epicenter: the point on the earth's surface directly above the location of an earthquake.

equal-area map: a map that preserves the area relationships between locations.

equator: the imaginary line around the earth halfway between the North and South Poles. The line divides the world into the Northern and Southern Hemispheres.

erosion: the gradual wearing away of rock or soil by water and wind.

evacuation: immediate and rapid movement of people away from danger.

evaporation: the process of a liquid heating up and changing into a gas, such as water vapor.

evergreen: a plant that keeps its leaves or needles throughout the year.

firebreak: a strip of cleared or plowed land used to stop the spread of a fire.

galaxy: a collection of star systems held together by gravity.

gelatinous: jelly-like.

geodesy: the study of the size and shape of the earth and the location of points on its surface.

geography: the study of the physical features of the earth and how human activity affects and is affected by these features.

geologist: a scientist who studies the solid and liquid matter that make up the earth and the forces that shape it.

geology: the scientific study of the history and physical nature of the earth.

geyser: a natural spring that shoots water into the air.

GIS: stands for Geographic Information System. A system for storing and manipulating geographical information on a computer.

GPS: stands for Global Positioning System. The system of satellites, computers, and receivers can determine the exact location of a receiver anywhere on the planet. It is used to determine location, speed, and direction.

GPS constellation: the movement and relationship of the 31 GPS satellites in space.

gravity: a force that pulls all objects toward the earth.

grid system: a type of city plan in which streets run at right angles to each other, forming a grid.

gyroscope: a spinning wheel or disk used to measure or maintain orientation.

high resolution: showing a lot of detail.

horizon: the line in the distance where the land or sea seems to meet the sky.

income: the amount of money someone makes.

infrared light: radiation that has longer wavelengths than visible light, and can be felt as heat by humans.

interpreter: someone who translates from one language to another.

irrigate: to supply land with water, usually for crops.

landmark: a manmade or natural object that is easily seen from a distance and can be used to find or mark a location.

Landsat: a satellite system operated by the U.S. government that studies and photographs the earth's surface.

landslide: when a mass of earth or rock slides down from a mountain or cliff.

latitude: a measure of distance from the equator, in degrees. The equator is 0 degrees. The North Pole is 90 degrees latitude north and the South Pole is 90 degrees latitude south.

legend: a key to all the symbols used on a map.

light year: the distance that light travels in one year, equal to about 5.88 trillion miles (9.46 trillion kilometers).

longitude: a measure of distance from the prime meridian, in degrees. The prime meridian is 0 degrees with lines running 180 degrees east and west from it.

magnet: something that attracts metal.

magnetic field: the invisible area around a magnet that pulls objects to it or pushes them away.

map projection: a flat map that represents the globe.

marine chronometer: a spring-loaded clock able to keep very precise time at sea.

Mercator projection: a map on which the lines of latitude and longitude cross at right angles, and the areas farther from the equator appear larger.

mercury: a liquid metal used inside thermometers.

Middle Ages: the name for a period of time from around 500 to 1400 CE. It is also called the Medieval Era.

mid-ocean ridge: an underwater mountain system.

military: the armed forces of a country.

Morse Code: an alphabet represented by combinations of long and short signals.

NASA: National Aeronautics and Space Administration. The U.S. organization in charge of space exploration.

National Oceanic and Atmospheric Agency (NOAA): a United States government agency focused on the condition of the oceans and the atmosphere.

nautical: relating to ships, shipping, sailors, or navigation on a body of water.

nautical chart: a visual representation of an ocean area and the nearby coastal regions.

navigate: to make your way from one place to another on water, air, or land, especially in a ship, aircraft, or vehicle.

navigation: figuring out locations and planning or following routes.

navigator: a person or device that navigates.

New World: North and South America.

ocean floor: the bottom of the ocean.

oceanographer: a scientist who studies the ocean.

optical: built to assist sight.

orbit: the path of an object circling another in space.

outer space: the physical universe beyond earth's atmosphere.

pacing: measuring a distance by walking it and counting the number of steps taken.

parallel: when two lines going in the same direction can continue forever and never touch, like an = sign.

pendulum: a weight hung from a fixed point that swings back and forth.

perimeter: the length of the line around something.

planet: a large body in space with an orbit around the sun.

plate tectonics: the scientific theory that describes the large-scale movement of the plates in the earth's crust.

Polaris: the North Star, which is almost directly over the North Pole.

pole: one end of a magnet.

politics: the business of governments.

population density: a measurement of the number of people in a given area, usually per square mile.

prime meridian: the imaginary line running from the North Pole to the South Pole through Greenwich, England. The line divides the world into the Eastern and Western Hemispheres.

radar: a system for detecting the presence of aircraft or other objects. It uses radio waves reflected from surfaces.

radiate: to spread outward.

radiation: energy transmitted in the form of rays, waves, or particles from a source, such as the sun.

radio navigation: the use of radio frequencies to determine one's position on the earth and navigate a ship or airplane.

radio wave: an electromagnetic wave used to transmit radio and television signals and for navigation.

radius: the distance from the center of a circle to every point along the edge of that circle.

receiver: a device that converts signals such as radio waves into sound or visual form.

repel: to resist or push away.

reservoir: a natural or manmade body of water stored for future use.

rhumb line: a line crossing all meridians at the same angle or bearing.

rover: a slow-moving vehicle used to explore planets.

satellite: an object that circles another object in space. Also a device that circles the earth and transmits information.

scale: the ratio of a distance on the map to the corresponding distance on the ground.

scarce: in short supply.

scholar: a person who is highly educated in a subject.

scuba: a container of air connected to a mouthpiece, used for swimming underwater. Stands for self-contained underwater breathing apparatus.

sediment: dirt, fertilizer, rocks, and other tiny bits of matter deposited in rivers and oceans.

sextant: a navigational instrument used to measure the angle between two objects, usually the horizon and a celestial body.

shoal: an area of shallow water.

slope: the slant of a surface with one end higher than another.

solar power: energy from the sun.

solar system: the collection of eight planets, moons, and other celestial bodies that orbit the sun.

sonar: a method of using sound pulses to detect objects and to measure the depth of water.

sounding line: a weighted rope used to measure sea depths.

Space Race: the competition between the United States and the Soviet Union to achieve the greatest accomplishments in space exploration.

spatial: viewed in a three-dimensional environment.

species: a group of plants or animals that are related and look like each other.

sphere: a round, three-dimensional object shaped like a ball.

star tracker: an instrument that logs star positions to aid in navigation.

submarine: under the surface of the sea. Also a ship that can dive deep underwater.

surveyor: someone who measures land areas to set up boundaries.

technology: tools, methods, and systems used to solve a problem or do work.

telescope: a tool used to see objects that are far away.

terrain: the physical features of land.

theory: an idea or set of ideas intended to explain something.

thermal vent: a groove in the earth's surface that emits very hot water heated from deep within the earth.

three dimensional: with depth, not just width and height.

topographic map: a map that uses large-scale detail to show both natural and man-made features, usually including elevation.

trade: the exchange of goods for other goods or money.

transpiration: the process by which a plant pulls water up through its roots, which then collects on its leaves and evaporates into the atmosphere.

triangulation: the process of determining location and distance to a point by measuring the angles of a fixed baseline of known length.

trilateration: the process of determining location by measuring distance between known objects.

tsunami: a very large ocean wave, usually caused by an earthquake.

universe: everything that exists everywhere.

vegetation: all the plant life in an area.

wet compass: a compass formed with a magnetic needle floating in water.

wetland: an area where the land is soaked with water, such as a swamp.

zenith: the point directly overhead in the sky.

RESOURCES

Books

Arnold, Caroline, *The Geography Book: Activities for Exploring, Mapping, and Enjoying Your World.* New York: John Wiley & Sons, Inc., 2002.

Borden, Louise, *Sea Clocks: The Story of Longitude.* New York: Margaret McElderry Books, Simon & Schuster Children's Publishing, 2004.

Dickinson, Rachel, *Tools of Navigation.* White River Junction, Vermont: Nomad Press, 2005.

Ganeri, Anita, *The Story of Maps and Navigation.* New York: Oxford University Press, Inc., 1997.

Gurney, Alan, *Compass: A Story of Exploration.* New York: W. W. Norton & Co., 2004.

Johnson, Sylvia, *Mapping the World.* New York: Atheneum Books for Young Readers, Simon & Schuster Children's Publishing, 1999.

Lasky, Kathryn, *The Man Who Made Time Travel.* New York: Farrar, Straus and Giroux, 2003.

Panchyk, Richard, *Charting the World: Geography and Maps from Cave Paintings to GPS.* Chicago: Chicago Review Press, 2011.

Petersen, Christine, *Colonial People: The Surveyor.* New York: Marshall Cavendish, 2011.

Ross, Val, *The Road to There: Mapmakers and Their Stories.* Plattsburgh, New York: Tundra Books, 2003.

Smith, A. G., *Where Am I? The Story of Maps and Navigation.* Buffalo, New York: Stoddart Kids, 1997.

Watts, Steve, *Make it Work! Maps.* Chicago: World Book, Inc., 1996.

Young, Karen Romano, *Small Worlds: Maps and Mapmaking.* New York: Scholastic, 2002.

Web Sites

Google Maps: www.maps.google.com

Google Mars and Google Earth for Mars www.google.com/mars and www.google.com/earth/explore/showcase/mars.html

Google Earth: www.google.com/earth

User Guide for Google Earth: serc.carleton.edu/sp/library/google_earth/UserGuide.html

Google Ocean: www.google.com/earth/explore/showcase/ocean.html

U.S. Geological Survey: www.usgs.gov

Landsat: landsat.usgs.gov and landsat.gsfc.nasa.gov

EarthNow! Landsat Image Viewer: earthnow.usgs.gov/earthnow_app.html?sessionId=2fb7f48c08a7657b5cfb24054c8ae16921415

Earthquakes in all states: earthquake.usgs.gov/earthquakes

NASA resources on space travel: www.nasa.gov

National Geographic Best Pictures of Earth: news.nationalgeographic.com/news/2009/04/photogalleries/best-pictures-of-earth/

Information on the Mars Rover: marsrovers.jpl.nasa.gov/home/index.html

Solar System: solarsystem.nasa.gov/index.cfm

NOVA Online Series, *Lost at Sea: The Search for Longitude*: www.pbs.org/wgbh/nova/longitude

GPS and the Environment: www.gps.gov/applications/environment

Cousteau Society: www.cousteau.org

42eXplore Maps: www.42explore2.com/maps.htm

Lewis and Clark Expedition: lewis-clark.org/content/content-channel.asp?ChannelID=62

INDEX